FOREWORD

This new edition of the 1984 book renders the work which received the Prix "Maréchal Foch" from the Académie française in 1985 in a new, updated format. Information which has come to light since 1984 has merely served to corroborate the main ideas of the first edition.

At the time of the German victory in 1940 Churchill realised that it would be necessary to organise a return to the continent. The success of such an operation hinged on the United Kingdom staving off invasion and winning the defensive air battle of Britain. Through sheer stoic, courageous steadfastness the English were able to pull the operation off with rapid assistance from the United States - once Roosevelt deemed that the world balance of power produced by Germany's string of successes between 1936 and 1940 had become intolerable. When the Germans invaded Russia in 1941 Stalin ordered fighting to resume on a new, natural second front which he had previously closed off through the German-Russian pact of August 1939. Battle preparations on this second front, an unprecedented heavy operation, represented a lynchpin of the war.

The attack by German ally Japan may well have led the United States to review its strategy on Europe but Roosevelt did not allow himself to be swayed from his "Germany first" strategy. The opportunity to implement the latter was provided by the Battle of Midway in June 1942, the first strategic victory, albeit defensive, which saw the first failure in the unbroken series of Axis power (Germany-Italy-Japan) victories since 1935. This opened the way for the second strategy victory of the war, this time offensive, which would result in the collapse of the Axis powers by carrying the conflict to the very heart of its main player: Germany. The "Overlord" European landing operation resulted in the liberation of the latter.

Failure was not an option for the "Overlord" operation since a second attempt would almost certainly be impossible. Its successful preparation and execution hinged not only on military resources but also a combination of other factors such as civil engineering, information, intelligence, diplomacy, "decoy" manoeuvres (diversionary tactics to fool the enemy), etc. This book documents and provides a concise, clear account of the latter.

INTRODUCTION

The green land of Normandy evokes the pleasures of life.

However, with the ruins of pillboxes behind the beautiful sandy beaches, steles in various languages, English, Polish, German, French, vast cemeteries with white, black or grey stones, carefully looked after, frequently visited, and with flowers placed faithfully on the graves, remind us that on this welcoming land a hard battle was fought over a three-month period from June 6 to August 20 1944.

In many ways, the Second World War was an impressive affair, with the lightning war fought by the tanks and Stukas, deportations by the million, armies encircled, bombing raids ravaging whole cities, naval confrontations across the Pacific, packs of submarines tailing 200 ships in the Atlantic, two cities destroyed in seconds in a nuclear flash. In comparison, the battle fought over a 500 sq km rectangle in Normandy seems of lesser importance.

In actual fact, this campaign fought in Normandy was the crucial battle of the war. The planning of it was central to strategy throughout the entire war. Its initial phase comprised a huge amphibious assault against an enemy who had spent the previous four years taking measures to prevent it. This exceptionally difficult military operation, the like of which had never been seen, demanded resources on a scale that ruled out any second attempt in the event of failure.

During the second phase, a fortunate tactical initiative put an end to the violent hand-to-hand fighting, opening the way for an advancing tide of destruction against the enemy forces. The success or failure of the battle was expected to decide the outcome of the greatest conflict in human history – and indeed it did so.

"Strategy is the art of combining the action of military forces with a view to achieving a war objective determined by the political power" (Larousse dictionary).

In terms of this definition, the battle of Normandy was the most genuinely strategic victory. It achieved the intimate blending of all categories of military forces existing at the time. It and nothing else could enable the Allied powers to achieve the political objective, namely to put an end to the Second World War by carrying the conflict into the very heart of Germany.

This is why, from 1940 to 1944, the strategic principle of giving priority to the defeat of Germany was asserted and gradually confirmed by the now Allied Nations. In order to implement this strategy, certain conditions had first to be met: victory in the Battle of the Atlantic and the weakening of German war machine.

Whilst working towards achieving these prerequisites, all the while, planning and preparations for the landing, the crowning feature of this strategy, went ahead.

The assault and the ensuing battle bloodied the soil of lower Normandy in the face of stout opposition from the German forces.

GENERAL JEAN COMPAGNON

6 JUNE 1944

THE NORMANDY LANDINGS

The strategic victory of World War II

Translation: 5/5

ÉDITIONS OUEST-FRANCE

13, rue du Breil, Rennes

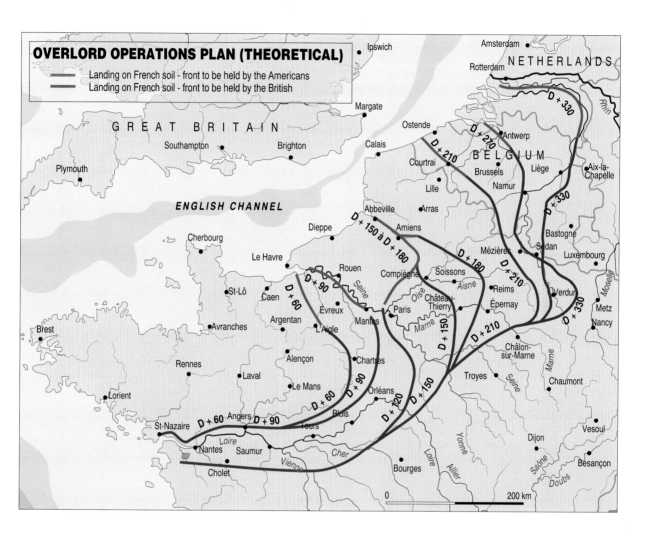

OVERLORD OPERATIONS PLAN (THEORETICAL)

— Landing on French soil - front to be held by the Americans
— Landing on French soil - front to be held by the British

The breakthrough at the end of this costly battle opened the way across France which would lead to peace.

Such is the framework of events to be related in the pages that follow – at the end of which a final toll and examination of the strategic consequences of the battle for Normandy will be set out.

Today, over fifty years after the battle, we hesitate in our minds between the tendency to forget, inspired by the calm beauty of Normandy restored, and emotion aroused by the evocation of the horrifying massacres and genocide. It is wrong to forget and emotion is useless. Better to come to a lasting awareness of the fact that the end to the holocausts necessarily involved the battle of Normandy.

Note: A few personal memories and thoughts on the events lived through and recounted by the author are brought together in a short postscript.

Quadrant Conference in Quebec (August 1943).
Mackenzie King, Roosevelt, W.Churchill in Quebec surrounded by members of the Combined Chiefs of Staff (C.C.S.): General Arnold,
General Portal, General A. Brooke, Admiral Leahy, General Sir J.Dill, General Marshall, Admiral King.
(R.H.A. document)

PART ONE

PRELIMINARIES
AND
PREPARATION

SUNDAY 10 AUGUST 1941.

The first meeting between Churchill and Roosevelt at Placentia Bay, Newfoundland, a base handed over for use by the United States in the terms of an exchange agreement between the United States and the United Kingdom (involved the delivery of 50 destroyers to England in exchange for the use of 7 bases in Newfoundland, Bermuda, the Caribbean and Guyana) concluded on 5 September 1941.

On 9 August, Churchill arrived on the cruiser the "Prince of Wales" for his first meeting with President Roosevelt on the American cruiser the "Augusta".

On the morning of 10 August, the American President, the British Prime Minister and their chiefs of staff attended a religious service conducted by two British and American padres with a congregation of several hundred sailors of both nationalities onboard the "Prince of Wales", the newest English cruiser in the fleet. The ship later sank off Singapore on the afternoon of 10 December 1941 after being hit by Japanese aircraft based in Indochina (near Saigon).

Churchill chose the hymns himself: "For those in peril on the sea", "Onwards Christian solders" and "Oh God our help in ages past", celebrated by Macaulay. Churchill wrote of the occasion: "The service was seen as a profoundly moving expression of the faith uniting our two peoples…". Over half of those that sang the hymns were to perish shortly afterwards.

In his 15 August press conference, President Roosevelt referred to this religious service as "a major historic moment".

The two great leaders saw in the affirmation of their Anglo-American spiritual and humanistic values a stark contrast to the values advocated by Hitler. This was also manifest in the Atlantic charter discussed in the following days and adopted on 12 August.

The Atlantic charter was a manifesto setting out the principles for a better world.

Paragraph 6 refers to the "destruction of Nazi tyranny". The very affirmation of a objective commonly held by a power at war, the United Kingdom and the United States, a country that was technically neutral appears incredible to us today. It was indicative of President Roosevelt's will to re-establish the world balance of power so disrupted by Germany.

CHAPTER ONE

WAR STRATEGY

GRADUAL MATURING OF ALLIED DECISIONS

« You will enter the continent of Europe and, in conjunction with other united nations, undertake operations aimed at the heart of Germany and the destruction of her armed force…»

These were the words used in January 1944 by the Allied Chiefs of Staff Committee to describe the mission given to General Eisenhower, who had been designated on 6 December 1943 by President Roosevelt as Supreme Commander of the Allied Expeditionary Forces. In its simplicity, this directive expressed the very purpose of the war. It was the outcome of a series of conversations, studies, decisions and realisations, and interallied actions. Ever since the spring of 1940, the idea of a return in force to the mainland of Europe had been fixed in the minds of all as inevitable, something that the Allied commanders would have to pull off, and Hitler to foil.

As early as June 1940, after Dunkirk and before the defeat of France, Churchill thought that it would be necessary to set foot on the Continent in order to crush Germany. It was then that he made the first steps of the long

Dunkirk beach at the end of May 1940. Surrounded French and English forces attempt to disembark for England.
(E.C.P.A. Document)

journey that would take Britain back across the Channel.

On 22 June, Hitler declared "England has been driven from the continent forever". The very next night, a British commando of 120 men carried out a raid on the sand dunes close to Boulogne.

In fact, in his hour of victory, Hitler had already made two serious mistakes that bore the seeds of his long-term defeat. One was circumstantial and recent, the other was deep-seated and already not new.

On 20 May 1940, German tanks had reached Abbeville, cutting off from the rest of France the Belgian, British and French forces committed in Belgium, henceforth doomed to destruction.

On 25 May, instead of letting this action of encircling and extermination develop around Lille, Arras, Calais and Dunkirk, Hitler ordered von Rundstedt's army group to stop their movement and to concentrate on Paris and the destruction of the French army.

There has been much debating as to whether the reason for this order was the concern to let the German tanks recover after the long march from the Ardennes to the Channel. However that may be, it was an order which made the evacuation of Dunkirk possible.

Between 28 May and 4 June, 250,000 men of the British Expeditionary Force escaped death or imprisonment and made it back to England. They would form the nucleus around which the British army would be rebuilt. The evacuation was masterminded by Admiral Ramsay, later to become naval attaché to Eisenhower in 1944. Among the leaders of the expeditionary corps evacuated from Dunkirk were corps commander General Alan Brooke, future British

Chief of Imperial General Staff (C.I.G.S.) from 1941 to 1945, division commander Montgomery, and Dempsey. Between Arras and Lille, one of the German armoured divisions stopped on the 29th by Hitler's order of the 25th was 7th Panzer Division under General Rommel. These same commanders would again come face to face in Normandy, some of them also having met in the meantime in Africa..

Hitler's second mistake was to have built up, at short notice it is true, his armed forces for a short land war. A combination of tanks and Stuka support aircraft had soon brought victory in Poland and in France. No thought had in fact been given to invading England, although the moment was favourable.

Without doubt the 350,000 men of the British Expeditionary Force evacuated from France via Dunkirk and Cherbourg were ready to oppose the invasion; but they had left their weapons and vehicles (82,000 vehicles, 2,300 guns) on the soil of France. Likewise, British fighter squadrons had lost over 400 planes in the aerial combats of 10 May to 20 June. But the German navy did not have the appropriate transportation for a landing, neither did it have the wherewithal to protect a large naval convoy. With 57 U-boats at the outset of war in 1939, whereas Admiral Dönitz commanding the submarine fleet calculated that he would require 300 to act effectively against Britain, they lost 17 during July 1940. The Luftwaffe's available fighters, 1,200 in number, could only just provide adequate air cover against 700 British fighters. But the bombers were short-range aircraft designed for ground support and could not reach the heart of England without redeploying on airfields set up on soil conquered in France, Belgium and the Netherlands.

This is why in June and July Hitler hoped - in vain - to obtain a concession to his ambition from Britain without having to invade. It was not until 16 July that he gave the order for the invasion to be carried out in mid-August. By then it was too late. Britain had had time to gather together her forces on land and particularly in the air; her defences were strengthened by excellent radar cover. Penetrating British air space proved extremely costly. The invasion was postponed until 27 September, leaving precious little time to exploit any landing before winter set in.

Meanwhile, the Germans' already too slender means of naval transportation had become a target for the British bombers.

On 17 September 1940, Hitler dropped the idea of invading Britain indefinitely. He gave orders to the German navy to concentrate its efforts against the merchant shipping between Britain and America: the battle of the Atlantic which was already underway was extended. Hitler ordered Goering to continue bombing England with growing intensity, with the ports as targets, and soon cities and industrial centres such as London and Coventry. He thus allayed suspicion whilst devoting himself to preparing the invasion of Russia with whom the alliance concluded in 1939 on the eve of the war was showing signs of strain.

Churchill on the other hand already anticipated that it would be one day necessary to return to the Continent. With the benefit of hindsight after the costly Dardanelles experiment during the First World War as to the tactical and technical difficulties of landing in strength, he knew that an operation of this nature cannot be improvised and involves lengthy preparation if it is to succeed.

As early as July 1940, he set up a "Combined Operations Command" at the head of which he put Admiral Keyes, later replaced, in October

250 000 British troops are successfully saved from Dunkirk leaving a great number of vehicles and equipment behind.
(E.C.P.A. Document)

1939: signing of the pact between Germany and Russia. By virtue of this agreement Hitler first of all put paid to Poland in the east in September 1939, then France in the west on June 1940. When in June 1940, Hitler invaded Russia, the second front which had existed in 1939 was no longer in place since it has disintegrated as a result of the peaceful truce in the east obtained by Hitler in the terms of the German–Russia pact. Stalin requested the opening of a second front from as early as July 1941. In the time it took to do so, however, Germany had considerably strengthened its military might. Before opening a second front it was necessary to stop the advance of the Axis powers at Midway, cut Germany off via the Mediterranean, win the Battle of the Atlantic and wear down German's fighting capacity via systematic bombing campaigns.
(E.C.P.A. Document)

1941, by Admiral Mountbatten. In October 1940, he assigned it to study the possibility of establishing a bridgehead in the Cotentin peninsula. The idea of this offensive was returned to several times until such time as it became possible to execute a larger scale landing.

Links between Great Britain and the United States were increased and tightened from July 1940 on. The close rapport between the two nations was the first reason for this. Also President Roosevelt was worried by the extension of German power and the threat that it brought to bear on world equilibrium. At the end of June 1940, England remained alone at war, needing as much help as possible within limits imposed by American neutrality. In July 1940, a mission of American naval and military observers came to England for exploratory conversations. One after the other, exchange and assistance measures were implemented, and also the loan of ships for the right to use bases on Commonwealth territory the world over, the supply of equipment to make up for losses sustained during the French campaign, installations in naval yards in the United States made available for the repair of merchant ships, later warships, the extension of the American security and patrol zone in the Atlantic... This assistance reached its climax on 8 March 1941 when the Lend-Lease Bill was passed by the American Senate.

In January 1941 secret talks on the defence of the Atlantic took place among Chiefs of Staff in Washington. It was then conceded that in the event of the war spreading to America and the Pacific, the Atlantic and Europe would be of decisive importance, and that destroying Hitler would be the number one priority. In March 1941, some American officers went to Britain to survey possible sites for air bases.

Thus in the months immediately following defeat in 1940 two essential concepts began to take shape:
– a full-scale return to the mainland of Europe;
– priority given to the defeat of Germany.

The invasion of Russia on 21 June 1941 would give a particular twist to the development of these two ideas.

Likewise with Hitler, it is interesting to note that the prospect of a return of the Anglo-Americans to the Continent was something that was constantly in the back of his mind. In September 1940, he cancelled his plans for invading England. He knew that for the time being he did not have the means to do so, and would only be able to go ahead with the idea when he had increased his naval and air strength. He then started to feel the by now unfriendly attitude of his Soviet ally,

11

whose pretensions in Romania threatened the Ploesti oil fields, free use of which was vital to Germany. Thanks to his available land army, with its powerful armoured contingent, he felt capable of crushing Russia within a few months, before Britain, probably joined by the United States, could intervene in the west. Once freed of the Russian threat he would weigh down with all his might against England who would then have to admit defeat. In July 1940 Hitler wrote the following sentences: "In the event that invasion [of England] does not take place, our efforts must be directed to the elimination of all factors that let England hope for a change in the situation. ... Britain's hope lies in Russia and the United States. If Russia drops out of the picture, America, too, would be lost for Britain because the elimination of Russia would greatly increase Japan's power in the Far East. ... Decision: Russia's destruction must therefore be made a part of this struggle. The sooner Russia is crushed the better. The attack will achieve its purpose only if the Russian State can be shattered to its roots with one blow. ... If we start in May '41 we will have five months in which to finish the job".

In July 1941, 20 days after the invasion of Russia, Hitler put the finishing touches to his strategy: "The military domination of Europe after the defeat of Russia will enable the strength of the Army to be considerably reduced in the near future. Naval armament must be restricted to those measures which have a direct connection with the conduct of the war against Britain and, if the case should arise, against America. The main effort in armament will be shifted to the Air Force, which must be greatly increased in strength."

Churchill anticipated the German attack against Russia. On 26 June 1940 he wrote: "If Hitler fails to beat us, he will probably recoil eastwards. Indeed he may even do this without trying invasion." In the course of the winter of 1940-1941, intelligence reinforced this opinion. From April 1941 on, Churchill was convinced by information in his possession on German troop movements of the imminence of an attack against Russia. On 3 April, he ordered his ambassador in Moscow, Sir Stafford Crips, to give Stalin a message informing him of these movements and the threat henceforth directed against the U.S.S.R. On 15 June, 5 days before Germany declared war on Russia, he

wrote to President Roosevelt: "From every source at my disposal, including some most trustworthy, it looks as if a vast German onslaught on Russia was imminent. ... Should this new war break out, we shall of course give all encouragement and any help we can spare to the Russians." At dawn on 21 June, German tanks crossed the Russian frontier. That same evening, in a speech broadcast over the B.B.C., Churchill declared: "We shall give whatever help we can to Russia and the Russian people. We shall appeal to all our friends and allies in every part of the world to take the same course." Ties were made between British and Soviet Chiefs of Staff. Material assistance began to be sent by the northern sea route. On 18 July, responding to 2 friendly messages sent by Churchill, Stalin expressed the wish to see the setting up of a second front, preferably in Northern France, while "realising the difficulties involved in the establishment of such a front".

Thus the problem of the second front was clearly posed; Churchill was not surprised. From June 1940, he had taken measures to envisage a landing on the continent of Europe in the long term. Pursuing the point further, and taking some account of Stalin's wishes, in September 1941, he ordered "the urgent completion of a draft plan of operations on the Continent, paying particular attention to requirements in special landing equipment and the appropriate training of troops."

From this moment, there appears what turned out to be a source of misunderstanding between the Soviet and British Allies: Stalin did not in fact realise the difficulties involved in an amphibious operation. For a year, Great Britain alone had borne the weight of the conflict in her skies, in the Atlantic and in Africa. To help Russia by sending in ships via Murmansk was possible, although difficult due to the German U-boat threat against the convoys. But to improvise a landing in the West, in the face of the forty or so divisions that Hitler had there permanently posted, was wishful thinking. The inevitable delays would be a cause of continual misunderstanding between Churchill and Stalin.

In fact, the second front already existed in 1939; if Russia had not made her alliance with him, Hitler would never have been able to concentrate all his forces against France; the second front would have existed and would not have needed to be recreated; the invasion of Russia in June 1941 would not have been possible. The German-Russian pact had given Hitler the chance to crush his enemies one by one.

The situation which thus came about meant that the problem of the formation of the second front was therefore now posed with its two aspects: the need to undertake it in order to close in and defeat Hitler's Germany, and attaining the preliminary conditions to its success. This second aspect involved a gradual approach that would make up the history of the three years that followed, and would settle the solution adopted to carry out the Normandy landing in June 1944.

The opening of hostilities between Japan and the United States marked the start of a new phase. Immediately after Pearl Harbour, Churchill and Roosevelt met in Washington in December 1941 at the Arcadia conference. This was the second conference of the Allied leaders, the first having taken place in August 1941 in Newfoundland and ending with the formulation of the "Atlantic Charter". Such meetings subsequently took place right through until the

Hitler inspecting the troops at Lorient.

end of the war, between Churchill and Roosevelt, and sometimes Stalin, each accompanied by their close advisers and Chiefs of Staff.

At this Washington meeting, the British were afraid they would find that the American leaders' interest in Europe had cooled now that the Japanese threat had grown in the Pacific. However Roosevelt and his Chief of Staff, General Marshall, immediately confirmed: "Notwithstanding the entry of Japan into the war, our view is that Germany is still the prime enemy, and her defeat is the key to victory. Once Germany is defeated, the collapse of Italy and the defeat of Japan must follow."

This was a brave statement for the United States president to make. Public opinion in America was disturbed by Japan's attack in the Pacific on 7 December 1941. This "Germany first" policy laid "the fundamental basis of joint strategy". The assault on Europe was the corollary: it then became an operation to be mounted by the British and Americans - and no longer by the British alone in collaboration with the U.S.S.R. A Chiefs of Staff Committee was set up between the two countries, and jointly with a plan for the build-up of

THE NORMANDY LANDINGS

American armed forces, it was arranged that American ground troops and bombers should gradually be sent over to England.

America had huge resources which consequently promised well for the future. But in fact, in January 1942, the Germany-Italy-Japan axis was at the height of its power. It was victorious everywhere, in Russia, in the Pacific, the Atlantic, the Mediterranean, in Africa and in Southeast Asia. Once this expansion had been stopped, regaining the freedom of the seas and adequate ship-building were prerequisites for a cross-Channel invasion - still a long way off.

In the Atlantic, the German U-boat fleet of 30 units in September 1939 passed 100 in December 1941. In January 1942, Allied shipping sunk by submarine attacks in the Atlantic reached

300,000 tons (including 200,000 in American waters), and kept on increasing throughout the year. In the Pacific, Japan went from strength to strength, even threatening Australia. Nevertheless, a plan code-named Sledgehammer for a limited landing (possibly in the Cherbourg peninsula) in the autumn of 1942, to shore up the possible collapse of the Russian army, came under study at the instigation of General Marshall. This limited operation was to be followed by a large-scale operation, Round-up, in the spring of 1943. For this purpose, Bolero, the build-up of American forces in Europe, would be carried out along with the increase of armed forces in the United States.

Events of June 1942 would dictate otherwise. The first half of 1942 had brought continued success for the Axis. Meanwhile, Albert Speer had been placed at the head of German industry and obtained production figures in aircraft, tanks and submarines, ammunition and petroleum products that grew from month to month (for example: 190 U-boats were manufactured in 1942 whereas the German navy had a total 55 in September 39 and 190 on 1 December 1941.)

The American naval victory at Midway, in mid-Pacific, on 4 June 1942, marks the turning point of the war. It was the first setback - and a major one at that - for the Axis powers. Until then they had known nothing but success, ever since the remilitarisation of the left bank of the Rhine in 1936, the invasion of Manchuria in 1932 and the invasion of Ethiopia. Midway was the first sharp check. Others would follow, at El-Alamein, the landing in French North Africa in November 1942, or Stalingrad in January 1943. Gradually the initiative passed to the Allies' side. The decline appeared on the horizon, but for the time being it was still a long way off. Powerful Germany would gain further successes in Africa and Russia.

A few days after Midway, on 20 June 1942, Tobruk fell and Egypt came under threat. The German army attacked southern Russia towards the Caucasus and its oil resources. The

Although the Dieppe landing operation was costly in terms of human lives it contained lessons which were to prove valuable to the success of the " Overlord " operation.
(R.H.A. document)

Allied tract dropped by the RAF over France providing news of the Canadian raid on Dieppe on 19 August 1942.

Middle East was threatened with a linkup of German forces coming from Russia and Africa possibly supported by Japanese naval forces in the Indian Ocean.

The Allies had to avert this threat immediately and take an initiative on a comparable scale in Europe so as to take the weight of the German attack off the Russians.

On 25 July 1942, after some tough negotiations between the British and Americans, it was decided to abandon the landing on the Continent and carry out a landing code-named Torch, in North Africa, by 30 October. This operation would have the advantage of liberating the Mediterranean, recovering all shipping that until then had had to take the long way round the Cape, threatening Europe from the south, drawing off German forces, lessening pressure on the Russian front to that extent, and removing the threat to the Middle East.

This threat to Western Europe would be further maintained by air attacks, measures of decoy deceptions[1], and commando raids such as at Dieppe in August 1942. This landing, so costly for the Canadians involved, confirmed the quality of the German defences and gave the Allies some useful indications as to their organisation. The German High Command placed it more on the level of an invasion than a raid with limited objectives. They overstated its failure, and became excessively confident in their own ability to resist assault.

Early in June 1942, General Eisenhower arrived in London to take command over the American forces in Europe, which was still very small with two divisions and a few air units, but projected to reach two million men and women. On arriving, he immediately took stock of the inadequacy of the Allied air and naval forces to launch even such a limited operation as Sledgehammer in safety and with any chance of success, for minimal advantage out of all proportion with the risks and effort involved. Hitler still had about forty divisions in the West. German U-boats in the Atlantic were sinking American oil-tankers close in to the coast of Florida, and decimating convoys carrying personnel and equipment to the British Isles. Gradually the convoys' defences became better organised, but while 21 U-boats were destroyed during the first quarter of 1942, the German shipyards produced 4 to 5 new submarines for every 1 sunk. At this point, General Eisenhower was named to command operation Torch, a landing in French North Africa to take place on 8 November 1942.

Marshall.
(U.S. Army document)

1. The term "decoy" (diversionary tactics) referred to in this book means actions designed to divert the enemy, i.e. give them misleading information in terms of its real intentions, provide incorrect information to its intelligence sources. In short "decoy" means giving the enemy the falsest possible idea vis-à-vis real operations.

Dieppe, 18–19 August 1942. Canadian commandos advance towards their objectives using tanks as cover.

Casablanca, 24 January 1943. General Giraud, President Roosevelt, General de Gaulle and Churchill Casablanca decide to continue the operations in the Mediterranean once the Tunisian campaign to put an end to the German presence in Africa was over. The decision was also taken to achieve, by 1943, the prerequisites for a successful landing operation on the continent in 1944, i.e.:
• winning the battle of the Atlantic.
• conducting the maximum numbers of air raids possible against Germany to deplete its industrial capacity.
They undertook to fight the war until the "unconditional surrender of the Axis Powers". Generals Giraud and de Gaulle are brought together.

In January 1943, Roosevelt and Churchill met at Casablanca. The decisions they then took, measures for implementation worked out by the Allied Chiefs of Staff Committee, marked a new, decisive stage in the preparation of the opening of the second front. Briefly, these were:

– operations on the European theatre would be carried out for the purpose of defeating Germany on the largest scale,

– after Tunisia (where the war was currently being waged), Sicily would be occupied so as to secure communications channels in the Mediterranean, to weigh down on Italy, and divert German pressure away from Russia,

– operations in the Pacific would be pursued within limits such that they would not hinder chances of inflicting final defeat on Germany in the event of a favourable opportunity arising,

– the destruction of German U-boats was an important task,

– the air offensive against Germany would be stepped up as far as possible,

– the most powerful available forces would be gathered in England to return to the Continent as soon as German resistance had been sufficiently weakened. For this purpose, the need was confirmed for an American force to be set up quickly in England capable of making the most of favourable August weather to conduct a *Sledgehammer*-type operation.

These decisions restated the strategic principle of giving priority to the defeat of Germany, in spite of doubts expressed by Chiefs of Staff as to the possibility of pulling off a large-scale landing (and not a limited *Sledgehammer*-type operation) before the spring of 1944. Indeed, the ongoing Mediterranean campaign had first to be completed with all possible gains made, namely the threat to Germany from the south, drawing off German divisions towards Italy,

Dieppe beach. Aftermath of the landing operation and costly retreat of the Canadian force on 19 August 1942.

and lastly the capture of airfields in the region of Rome, which would enable the bombing of the Ploesti oil fields in Romania.

The main thing was to achieve all the necessary prerequisites for a cross-Channel invasion. These were:

– to win the battle of the Atlantic against the German U-boats (in November 1942 Allied sinkings bottomed out at 600,000 tons),

– having thus regained the freedom of the seas, to gather in England a force of at least 40 divisions with the possibility of bringing in another 60 from the United States,

– to decrease German industrial capacity, then still on the increase, by an aerial bombing campaign.

The Casablanca conference added a declaration of principle to these concrete decisions: the war would be continued relentlessly until the *unconditional surrender* of the enemy powers. This declaration is understandable. It is a statement of Anglo-American determination and confidence in their strength. It was also an assurance given to Stalin that the possible inability to open the second front in 1943 would not mean that the idea had been abandoned, and that no separate negotiation would ever take place with Hitler or any other German authority. It did however present a

Franklin Delano Roosevelt, President of the United States.

Admiral Leahy, General Giraud, Commanders Viret and Beaufre, President Roosevelt, General Marshall, Commandant Poniatowski (July 1943, Washington). General Giraud establishing the terms and conditions for re-arming and deploying the French forces with the American authorities during his visit to the United States in July 1943.
(E.C.P.A. Document)

serious drawback. For the army and the German people it meant that there was no way of escaping Hitler's destructive folly. It gave Goebbels an invaluable propaganda weapon to carry on the war to the end. It discouraged in advance, or at least weakened any German attempts at resisting Hitler by offering them no future. Leaving the German people with no alternative to a hopeless struggle, such a declaration was likely to prolong the war. This was undoubtedly the case.

The commander-in-chief of the operation for the return to Europe was not designated. Initially, due to the preponderance of British forces, it seems to have been envisaged that he should be British. By now, with the increase of mainly ground and air forces coming from United States, it appeared more appropriate that an American general should be appointed.

After the Casablanca conference, the prerequisites for invasion, the freedom of the seas and strategic air bombing, were to be researched and carried to the level of the general conduct of the war by the Allied Chiefs of Staff Committee. The preparation of the actual landing itself would be entrusted to a special Anglo-American staff.

CHAPTER TWO

LONG-TERM

PREPARATIONS

General Morgan, appointed Chief of Staff to the Supreme Allied Commander (C.O.S.S.A.C.) on 12 March, immediately started work on planning the "Overlord" operation. A directive that he received from the allied Combined Chiefs of Staff on 25 May 1943 stipulated that the military might "deployed in the beachhead" would be 29 American, British and Canadian divisions plus one French division. The 2nd armoured division (General Leclerc) was assigned to the mission at the end of March 1944.

Left:
Propaganda poster from 1944.

On 12 March 1943, British General F. Morgan was appointed *Chief Of Staff to Supreme Allied Commander* (C.O.S.S.A.C.). On 26 April 1943 he received a general directive. The purpose being to defeat the German forces in the north-west of Europe, his brief was to draw up plans for three types of possible operations:

– *Starkey*: a diversionary operation in 1943 to fix enemy forces in the west and to prevent the Germans from reinforcing in Russia and Italy.

– *Rankin*: a return to the continent at short notice in the event of German collapse.

– *Overlord*: a full-scale assault in 1944 as early as possible.

On 25 May 1943, COSSAC was given a supplementary directive regarding Overlord by the Allied Chiefs of Staff Committee:

Object: to secure a foothold on the Continent from which further offensive operations could be developed. For this purpose, to seize port facilities to enable the arrival of follow-up shipments directly from the United States (at the rate of 3 to 5 divisions per month).

Target date: May 1944.

Project to be submitted by 1st August 1943.

Assault forces: 29 divisions (plus a probable French one), including: initial landing 5 divisions plus 2 divisions for the immediate follow-up.

For *Starkey*, plans reached quite an advanced stage. Indeed, COSSAC's orders, in the absence of a real landing, were nevertheless to carry out an exercise intended to deceive the enemy, to provoke his reactions and to maintain the threat. This exercise took place on 8 September 1943. It involved the assembling of landing-craft in southeast England around Southampton with troops embarking and setting up convoys. Its purpose was to feint a landing across the straits of Dover towards the Pas-de-

Calais, the shortest crossing. This was a delicate arrangement since it had to attract the Luftwaffe's attention without the surrounding population having to suffer extra bombing raids. It had to be interrupted fairly quickly, then immediately presented to the press, not as a failure, but for what it actually was, an exercise. It had nevertheless to last enough long for

the Allied air force and underground resistance fighters to observe German reactions: infantry units alerted, anti-aircraft artillery, coastal batteries and any movement of reserves. It had to avoid any compromising exposure of the Belgian and French resistance or raising their hopes too high. On the other hand, this exercise confirmed the German command in the idea that the threat of Allied invasion lay first and foremost in the Pas-de-Calais sector.

19

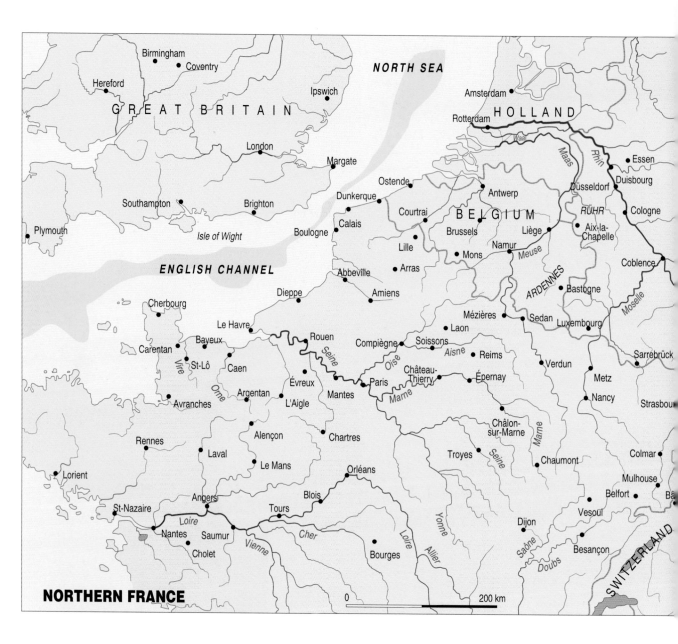

NORTHERN FRANCE

0   200 km

For *Rankin*, opportunistic landings in the event of a German collapse could be derived at short notice from *Overlord* in its current state of preparation. It was therefore on *Overlord* that COSSAC concentrated his attention and research. He took into account work and experiments already carried out by the British heads of combined operations since October 1941 under Admiral Mountbatten: reconnaissance missions along the coast of Europe from Norway to Bayonne; landings carried out in Norway at Lofoten and Vaagso in 1941, at Saint-Nazaire, Boulogne, Dieppe, Le Casquet, Sainte-Honorine and Sark in 1942; research and manufacture of special landing equipment such as landing-craft, amphibious tanks and elements for the artificial ports.

The first two vital problems to be resolved were:

  – the choice of landing site,

  – deciding on how many forces to commit in the light of the resources available for transporting and landing them by air and sea.

Later on, air support, naval support, appraisal of enemy forces and their capacity to react, the manoeuvre to be carried out on land, holding and consolidating the beachhead etc, would have to be studied. These areas were dealt with in the plan prepared by COSSAC but they would be the responsibility of the Commander-in-Chief himself once he had been appointed. The appropriate decisions would be taken then.

The choice of landing site was left totally free to COSSAC whose mission was to draw up plans for a full-scale assault on the Continent. The entire coast from Norway to Portugal could therefore be envisaged. However some possible options were immediately ruled out.

Jutland and the Friesian coast were unfavourable to present day armies whose offensive capacity lay in their large numbers of tanks and vehicles. Moreover, they had no decent ports.

The choice was therefore restricted to the coasts of the English Channel, and along this section, two zones, the Pas-de-Calais-Somme and lower Normandy. COSSAC had these two possible options thoroughly analysed by two teams from staff headquarters.

Being closer to England, the northern zone, in the Pas-de-Calais-Somme area, had some undoubted advantages: it was the shortest sea crossing; the shortest distance by air, thus allowing maximum presence for a given

S.A.S. parachutists in training at Ringway.
(R.H.A. document)

The Iberian peninsula, where the second front was opened against Napoleon, was too far from Germany but most of all too lacking in communications to enable a rapid advance.

Norway was considered by Hitler as a possible Allied landing site. The Führer declared in January 1942: "Norway is a decisive zone for the outcome of this war. Her defence will be under my direct command." However, for the Allies, it offered no easy way into Germany.

number of flying hours; closeness to Germany and the Ruhr, the heart of German industrial power; it had sea approaches and favourable beaches, at least near Calais and Boulogne, because further south the cliffs of Picardy towered over the beaches and directed the beach exits to the hinterland. Two large ports fairly close by, Le Havre and Antwerp, could be captured in quick time to allow supplies to be brought through to the battle that would take place after the landing, in the direction of Germany. Many factors worked in favour of this sector. But the Germans could also read the map, and were likely to be most prepared for an invasion on the very part of the coast from which they themselves had planned to embark on the conquest of England in 1940. This was the most heavily fortified zone, with the greatest troop density (15 divisions). The short distance to Germany would favour the action of short-range fighters and the commitment of reserves. However the build-up from the conquered beaches was bound to be slow and the days and hours immediately following the landing would be the most vulnerable ones.

Lower Normandy between the Vire and the Dive rivers offered easy-to-reach sandy beaches, and sea approaches of comparable value. The beach exits were straightforward; but beyond towards Caen and from there southwards it was open country, easy to cross; further to the west, the bocage, consisting of small hedged fields and sunken lanes, favoured the defender and was likely to slow down the widening of the bridgehead towards Saint-Lô and Alençon. The ports of Brest and Cherbourg were nicely placed later on to receive shipping arriving directly from United States. However, Cherbourg, the closer of the two, was situated at the tip of a peninsula of bocage country, and separated from the beaches of lower Normandy by marshland at the mouth of the Vire, all factors that could delay its capture. The distance from England was greater here, but this disadvantage would be offset by maritime and naval supremacy without which no landing could be contemplated anyway. Whatever the broad strategy chosen, the road to Germany, the ultimate objective, would be longer; on the other hand this had the advantage of hindering the intervention of air support and German land troop reserves who over long distances would have to face attack from the Allied air forces and guerrilla actions by the French Forces of the Interior. Finally the lower Normandy sector could easily be cut off by aerial bombing raids along the Seine and the Loire.

From the meteorological standpoint - visibility, wind, rainfall - conditions were more or less the same in both the Picardy and lower Normandy areas.

In June 1943 COSSAC came out in favour of lower Normandy, basing all subsequent research on this choice.

An assessment of the available landing facilities showed that three divisions could be landed in the first wave, to be immediately followed by two brigades or tank groups. Two parachute divisions were planned but there was doubt as to how they were to be shipped across. COSSAC calculated that 18 divisions should have been landed by D + 14, and that 14 airfields would have been captured and made operational on French soil. The capture of Cherbourg was unlikely in such a short period because the Cotentin peninsula was separated from the beaches of lower Normandy by the valley of the Vire and the marshes around Carentan. However, given the allocated resources, there was no question of any landing taking place west of Carentan, at the neck of the Cotentin peninsula.

This raised the problem of how to maintain the bridgehead for two weeks, and maybe even longer, merely from the conquered beaches. The idea of creating an artificial port was an attractive one but the technology did not exist, at least not yet.

On 15 July 1943 COSSAC submitted his project for the landing before the Allied Chiefs of Staff Committee. In his preamble, he drew attention to 4 points:

– the need to ensure logistical back-up from the beaches after the landing (prior to capturing the natural harbours which might take a long time) and failing that through artificial ports for which no means existed,

– the need for invasion resources over and above those currently planned (inadequate air and sea transport),

– the need to create a favourable situation at the time of the landing by launching operations without further delay: measures of deception, using the air force and the forces of the interior to cut off communications, gather intelligence methodically, etc.,

– the need to understand the fundamental difference between *Overlord* and the landings in North Africa and Sicily.

Hitler and von Rundstedt.
(E.C.P.A. document)

The Quebec conference (*Quadrant*) in August 1943 brought together Roosevelt and Churchill, their advisers and Chiefs of Staff of the three armies of either country. It examined and approved the COSSAC project. It ordered COSSAC to proceed henceforth with the planning and preparation of *Overlord* taking into account the following remarks:

– the estimated numbers of troops brought ashore after the initial landing (on D + 14: 18

divisions and 30 operational squadrons on 14 terrains) were over-optimistic,

– a landing in the South of France was also envisaged,

– Churchill had expressed the wish that the initial assault forces be increased by 25%,

– the already major problem of insufficient landing resources was thus aggravated. No measure had been envisaged to solve this problem and satisfy Churchill's wish,

– research and production of methods for landing on the beaches were to be stepped up; and also methods of creating artificial ports,

– in conclusion *Overlord* was confirmed as the supreme operation of 1944 (planned date: May).

As a result, the COSSAC headquarters, which hitherto had had no more than a planning role, became operational. It came under the authority of *Combined Chiefs of Staff* with executive powers.

This change involved 4 areas of decision-making:

– a precise assessment of landing resources and how to achieve them,

– designating amphibious assault divisions to start training,

– organising security and secrecy around the mounting of the operation,

– ordering operations and special services (gathering intelligence, deception and intoxication directly for the benefit of *Overlord*).

During the second half of 1943 the direct preparation of *Overlord* was pursued in these 4 directions.

The COSSAC headquarters took on an operational form on the lines of American staffs. British officers were initially in the majority, but gradually Americans took over. Although the Supreme Commander had not been appointed, it was acknowledged that he should be American and it was everyone's impression that General Marshall would be named to command this the capital operation of the war, having held down the difficult job of Army Chief of Staff to President Roosevelt in Washington since 1939. In November 1943 Air Marshall Leigh-Mallory and Admiral Ramsay, both British, were named Chiefs of the Allied Expeditionary air and naval Forces, respectively. The ground troops that were to make up U.S. First

Phoenix support structure under construction.
(Photo taken from archive footage filmed by the British admiralty in 1943.)

Army were placed under the command of General Bradley, who reached his H.Q. at Bristol on 12 September 1943 coming from Sicily where he had commanded U.S. II Corps.

The ways and means of creating an artificial port, a protective dike, mooring caissons, floating quays etc., were examined in various places, at Combined Operations headquarters, in British shipyards and docks, arsenals etc. In August 1943 Sir Harold Wernher coordinated the whole research programme and submitted his overall project at the *Quadrant* conference. From then on, this plan was followed in all subsequent research and realisations. These involved dividing the work amongst many shipyards across Britain and the United States, estimating requirements in raw materials, steel, concrete, etc., with extra secrecy surrounding these projects, which were deliberately scattered for this reason. Shipping the parts across the Channel and assembling the whole were planned well ahead of the time. This enormous task was organised immediately after the Quebec conference. It involved naval forces, land armies, the Ministry of Labour, merchant navy administrations and the Ministry of Transport and Industry in both England and America. In January 1944, Sir Harold Wernher was able to assert that project implementation was well under way. In the end, 1,000,000 of tons of steel, cement, pontoon and jetty would take to sea from England to build the artificial ports at Arromanches and Saint-Laurent.

Another project to be set up was Operation P.L.U.T.O. - a *Pipe Line Under The Ocean* placed on the sea-bed across the Channel to Cherbourg. It was tested in the Severn estuary between Swansea and Ilfracombe. The results were disappointing, so tanker-barges to be towed across the Channel were added to the plan.

Also during the course of the second half of 1943, the research and development of armoured equipment and amphibious vehicles, as well as special contrivances devised by the beach engineers, went ahead briskly.

In November 1943, 7 combat-hardened divisions (4 U.S. and 3 British) with experience of seaborne landings were brought back from Italy and Africa to make up the well-trained hard core of the invasion force.

On the other hand the wish expressed by Churchill in Quebec for a 25% increase in the initial assault forces, with a corresponding increase in landing equipment, was not even brought up for study, much less for implementation.

Links with the Resistance in France and in Belgium were important both for gathering intelligence and for preparing operations during and after the landing. They went ahead briskly in 1943 but it is difficult to make even a rough assessment of them. Indeed there were countless exchanges in both directions and the methods used were equally varied, American and British organisations, French resistance movements, numerous underground networks, and also actions directed by the provisional government in Algiers. But this was also the year when the networks were decimated. Suffice it to remember, so as to situate them in relation to COSSAC's activities interspersed with the *Quadrant* conference at Quebec on 29 August, a few events that occurred in France, together with their dates. On 9 June 1943 General Delestraint, head of the Secret Army, was arrested in Paris shortly after returning from London. On 21 June, Jean Moulin was arrested in Caluire near Lyons. At the same time, Henri Fresnay, head of the "Combat" movement, J.-P. Lévy, founder of "Franc-Tireur", Emmanuel d'Astier de la Vigerie, head of "Libération-Sud", were on a mission to London. Passy, head of the B.C.R.A., and Pierre Brossolette's "Brumaire Arquebuse" mission to France took place in February 1943. It was on 18 September 1943 that Pierre Brossolette, accompanied by the Briton Yeo-Thomas, returned to France for his second and final mission. Yeo-Thomas got back to England in November 1943 (on the 15th). After failed attempts to return in December 1943 and January 1944, Pierre Brossolette was arrested on 4 February 1944. Political activities and resistance activities (intelligence and action) often closely overlapped. There were frequent exchanges between Britain and the continent; these were sometimes slow, sometimes fast, sometimes direct, sometimes tortuous. It is therefore difficult to quantify them with any precision. At any rate, they made a sizable contribution to the preparation of *Overlord*, mainly tthrough providing intelligence.

German propaganda designed to divide the allies.

CHAPTER THREE

ACHIEVING

THE PREREQUISITES

The conduct of the war at sea and in the air was the responsibility of the Allied Chiefs of Staff Committee in line with decisions taken in January 1943 at Casablanca. To achieve the preliminary conditions required for the success of Overlord, it involved two main areas: gaining the freedom of the seas through victory in the battle of the Atlantic, and reducing German manufacturing potential by strategic bombing raids over Germany.

The battle of the Atlantic began back in September 1939. Between this date and July 1940, the German navy lost about fifteen U-boats. The availability of French coasts and bases at Brest, Lorient and La Pallice had greatly facilitated German U-boat attacks on British convoys bringing resources vital for England's survival from America. A few figures illustrate this tremendous battle that would not swing in the Allies' favour until 1943. In September 1939,

German submarine at Lorient.

the German navy had a fleet of 51 U-boats of which 30 were operational. By the end of 1942 it had 400 including over 200 in Atlantic. Allied tonnage sunk certifies to the bitterness of this battle. Until April 1942, it stayed at an average 300,000 tons per month. In May 1942, it reached 451,000 tons; during a single convoy, 41 boats were sunk by 6 German submarines. In November 1942, the Torch expedition only reached the African coast intact because it was given an escort and air and naval cover to the detriment of other convoys, of which 650,000 tons was sunk. The decision taken at Casablanca in January 1943 to exert the greatest efforts in the anti-submarine struggle was justified. To recover supremacy on the seas was an indispensable prerequisite if a force of over a million men with their equipment was to be sent to England. With aircraft carrier escorts, the improvement of radar, asdics and other air

cover, life became increasingly difficult for the German U-boats.

The turning point was reached in May 1943. Whilst the German navy had lost 87 submarines in the course of the twelve months of 1942, in the single month of May 1943 it lost 41, in July 1943 37, and in August 1943, 20. Out of 12 tanker submarines enabling U-boats operating over long distances to refuel at sea off the coast of America, 9 were lost in August 1943 and the last one went missing in April 1944. This last date shows how the battle remained fierce until the end of the war. After the "black month" of May 1943, Admiral Dönitz prevailed upon Hitler to order the construction of 40 new U-boats a month. He modified the tactics of submarine attack, had them modernised by installing *schnorkels* enabling the batteries to be recharged under the surface. He began production of two new submarine models, one the small, 200 ton 23-type, the other the long-range high speed (17 knots) 21-type. The 23-type would operate in February 1945 along the coasts of Britain, and on 8 May 1945, 61 submarines of this type were ready for service in the German arsenals. As for the 21-type submarine, the first of these was launched on 30 April 1945, and 100 were then ready to leave the shipyards. It was thus only at the cost of continuous dogged battling that the forces required to execute *Overlord* could be shipped across to England. During the first four months of 1944, German U-boat sinkings again rose to 120,000 tons per month, but this figure was insignificant compared with the rate at which the Americans were now producing their Liberty-Ships.

The reduction of German war potential also resulted from a decision taken at Casablanca both to help the Russians as well as advance the *Overlord* operation. For that purpose, from March 1943 American 8th Air Force based in England would take part in the bombing offensive over Germany carried out by the British since 1941.

By the end of 1943, 8th *Air Force* numbered almost 1,000 bombers. This aerial battle over Germany was also a very hard-fought one, its prime target being the fighter factories so as to clear the skies of those planes. But the Allied bombers had to penetrate ever deeper into Germany to reach the industrial centres. These unescorted daylight fighter missions were extremely costly. In October 1943, *8th Air Force* carried out a bombing mission with 228 bombers on the ball-bearing production centre at Schweinfurl at a cost of 62 planes destroyed, 138 damaged and the loss of 599 American airmen. Without doubt, this bombing campaign had a powerful effect on German morale and wreaked havoc on communications networks. The actual drop in industrial capacity is a lot less easy to assess, and the figures quoted above with respect to U-boat production prove that manufacturing potential remained high. In other areas it was the same story. Monthly tank production was 120 in June 1940, and 1,200 in December 1943; aircraft production went from 600 in June 1943 to 1,700 in December 1943. German industrial capacity worked at full steam throughout the year 1943 under the efficient direction of Albert Speer, who had been minister since February 1942. So by the end of 1943 this was another area where requirements for launching the invasion in the spring of 1944 had only barely been met.

Also at the end of 1943, from 27 to 30 November, Churchill, Stalin and Roosevelt met at Tehran, the final meeting taking place on Churchill's 69th birthday. As we have just seen, although much improved, the general war situation was nevertheless still finely balanced. In the Pacific, the Japanese had been stopped, which left the Americans free to bring their very considerable resources to bear in Europe. The battle of the Atlantic had swung in the Allies' favour since the previous June. But militarily and industrially, Germany remained very strong. Concentrating on herself, and with the ability to execute timely withdrawals on the

German submarine returning from sea.

Admiral Dönitz addressing submarine crews at Lorient.
(German archives.)

**The railway bridge
at Tours destroyed
by allied aircraft.**
(E.C.P.A. document)

C.f. appendices: 1 (*The Battle of the
Atlantic*), 2 (*Damage to German industry
caused by Allied bombing in 1943*), 3
(*Dieppe & commando operations in Europe*),
4 (*Table of the main events leading up to the
landing in Europe*), p154-157.

Eastern front, she could hold on long enough to develop her new weapons and this time place the war once and for all on a victorious footing. Indeed in Russia, since February 1943, the situation was much improved, but not decisively so. Stalin therefore needed assistance: he wanted the opening of the second front without which the defeat of Germany was not possible. But then, if this landing code-named Overlord was a success, it would bring about not only an end to German hegemony, but peace, or to put it another way, the aftermath of war.

From then on, for "the Big Three" at Tehran, the prime concern was with winning the war but also even now with winning the post-war peace, or at least pushing forward their pawns in the direction of the political objectives of this period. This being so, the execution of *Overlord*,

about which Churchill appeared still somewhat undecided - that at least was the impression Stalin got -, was the crux of the matter. Stalin insisted on the Supreme Commander being appointed. The presence of a Supreme Commander in charge would convince him that the opening of the second front would indeed take place in May 1944 and that all necessary measures would be coordinated and carried out. A Soviet offensive would be launched on the eastern front in conjunction with *Overlord*.

For months Roosevelt had planned on entrusting the command, a heavy burden but which carried the historic decision of the war, to General Marshall, who had been moreover for 5 years the architect of American strategy and in achieving the necessary force to implement it. When the time came to take his decision, Roosevelt decided that he could not do without General Marshall at his side to see the war through to the end. On his way home to the United States, in Cairo on 5 December, he asked Churchill if he would accept Eisenhower to command the Allied forces and carry out the vital mission of the return into Europe. Churchill gave his assent. Stopping off in Tunis, Roosevelt informed Eisenhower of his decision, on 6 December 1943.

Until then, the idea of opening a second front had dominated war strategy; from now on, after being just an idea *Overlord* was to become a reality.

Eisenhower.
(U.S.I.S. document)

LE COMMANDEMENT ALLIE

VOICI VOS FRERES D'ARMES

Le général Eisenhower a fusionné les armées alliées en une seule force combattante.

L'adjoint du général Eisenhower, l'Air Chief Marshal britannique Tedder.

Voici, en conférence au Q.G. du Commandement Suprême Interallié, les hommes qui mèneront à l'ouest l'assaut contre la forteresse européenne de Hitler. Leur tâche ardue a été un travail sans égal de préparation, de stratégie et d'action coordonnée. Aujourd'hui, les forces qu'ils commandent comprennent l'armée, la marine et l'aviation les mieux entraînées du monde. De gauche à droite : le général Bradley, commandant les forces terrestres américaines ; l'amiral Ramsay, commandant les forces navales alliées ; Air Chief Marshal Tedder, adjoint au Commandant Suprême ; le général Eisenhower, Commandant Suprême ; le général Montgomery, commandant le groupe des armées britanniques ; Air Chief Marshal Mallory, commandant l'aviation alliée ; le général Smith, chef d'Etat-Major au Q.G. du Commandement Suprême.

Le général Eisenhower et Air Chief Marshal Tedder dirigent en Angleterre les préparations de la libération.

Le général Montgomery s'entretient avec ses troupes qui briseront les armées allemandes en Afrique.

Le général Walter Bedell Smith, chef d'Etat-Major.

L'amiral Alan G. Kirk, commandant la flotte de ligne américaine.

Air Chief Marshal Leigh-Mallory, commandant l'aviation alliée.

Le général Omar Bradley, commandant les troupes américaines.

Le général Carl A. Spaatz, commandant l'aviation américaine.

L'amiral Sir Bertram Ramsay, chef des forces navales.

CHAPTER FOUR

THE OVERLORD

COMMAND

Officially designated on Christmas Eve 1943 as Supreme Commander of the Allied Expeditionary Forces in Europe, General Eisenhower left the Mediterranean for Washington on 1st January, returning to London on the 14th.

In Washington, President Roosevelt informed him of past and future operations, and also of possible plans for the occupation of Germany after the war. General Marshall dealt with the preparation and the execution of Overlord with him. There was profound agreement between the two generals. In 1940, Eisenhower returned from the Philippines after a spell that had lasted six years alongside General MacArthur, then responsible for setting up an autonomous Filipino force. He was assigned to various commands of increasing importance as the U.S. Army went through its extraordinary expansion during 1941. At the time of Pearl Harbour, in December, he was Chief of Staff with U.S. Third Army. Four days later, he received a telegram ordering him to return to Washington immediately. Wishing to take full advantage of his deep knowledge of the Philippine Islands, which the Japanese were certainly going to attack, Army Chief of Staff General Marshall posted him to the War Plans Division at General Staff Headquarters.

Since the start of 1941, the War Plans Division had been preparing the expansion of the U.S. Army according to the Victory programme and according to the strategic concept of priority given to victory over Germany in the event of the United States entering the war against Japan and Germany. Within the ranks of this Division there was a prominent personality, Lieutenant-Colonel, later General Wedemeyer. During the years 1936-1938, Wedemeyer had studied at the German War School, the Kriegsakademie; he knew the German army well; he had seen the

Germans develop their doctrine of the use of tanks, and was familiar with Haushofer's strategic and geopolitical concepts on the importance of the continental heart of Nations. He had made an important contribution to the assessment of the American army to be raised, nearly 9 million men, including the Air Force, from an existing operational force estimated in May 1940, in a written report to President Roosevelt, at 5 divisions totalling 80,000 men, with enough equipment to fit out 500,000, and with a few hundred supporting aircraft. (As it turned out, by May 1945 American air and land forces had increased to 8,291,336 men.) Wedemeyer also undoubtedly played a part in the decision taken by Roosevelt early in 1941 to seek first of all victory over Hitler, who represented the greatest danger for the balance of world power.

On taking over as head of the War Plans Division, Eisenhower found a programme that had already received its broad outline - the expansion of the U.S. land army and air force through truly enormous industrial power -, and been partially implemented. He himself had just made an important contribution to training the newly created units, through selective National Service, which had been adopted in principle back in September 1940 for men of between 21 and 35 years of age.

Well groomed to deal with world problems after 6 years, from 1928 to 1934, spent working with the Undersecretary of State for Defence, Eisenhower soon became head of the Operations Division at general headquarters; reports piled up on his desk of defensive operations in which American forces were engaged, mainly in the Pacific which he knew so well, along with long-term plans for offensive operations that would allow considerably increased forces in the air, at sea and on land.

Left:
The Allied command.

It was within this Division that the strategic philosophy of the war was settled immediately after the Japanese attack. The enemy in Europe was to be destroyed first; his accomplice in the Pacific would follow.

Only in Europe could the efforts of the three Allies, Russia, Britain and the United States, be brought together. Pursuing in this direction, the Operations Division under Eisenhower came to the conclusion that a full-scale cross-Channel assault would have to be launched from England as its operational base. For such an operation to succeed, considerable superiority in the air was vital. General Marshall approved this verdict. He submitted it to President Roosevelt and convinced him that it was the correct one. In London that April, accompanied by Lieutenant-Colonel Wedemeyer, he strove to get Churchill and British Chief of the Imperial General Staff Alan Brooke to endorse his view. He remained firmly attached to this strategic conception and secured its acceptance. He then appointed Eisenhower in June 1942 to take command in England of the "American forces in Europe in the process of being built up and whose mission would be the American contribution to the return to the mainland of Europe. From his arrival, Eisenhower noted that troops, aircraft, ships and landing-craft were in too short supply to envisage launching any operation of this type in the near future. German forces in Western Europe were still vastly superior to any currently available in England, with fifty divisions in constant presence. Only a landing in North Africa could be reasonably envisaged, and this operation was recommended by the British; Eisenhower was won over to the idea and placed in command. Consequently, on his return to London 18 months later, in January 1944, he came back to the mission he himself had prepared earlier in Washington. Meanwhile he had commanded Allied landings in North Africa, Sicily and Italy, where he had shown fine tactical sense and amassed a wealth of experience in handling men in combat; he had invented a style of inter-allied command

"Overload" air force chiefs pictured with General Eisenhower. From left to right: General Brereton, General Vandenberg, Air Marshall Coningham, Air Marshall Leigh-Mallory.

**Montgomery pictured
when he was a Marshall.**
(E.C.P.A. document)

Ramsay, who had already commanded the British naval forces for the possible landing envisaged for 1942, and thus had an opportunity to work with Eisenhower. He was familiar with the Channel, having been the architect of the Dunkirk evacuation in June 1940. The air forces commander-in-chief for Overlord was Air Chief Marshall Leigh-Mallory, a veteran of the air battle of Britain.

As his deputy, General Eisenhower insisted on having British *Air Marshall* Tedder, an eminently competent, well-liked and respected airman who had been with him in the Mediterranean. The understanding between the two chiefs was perfect. Tedder brought his considerable influence to bear and used his position to good effect, especially in dealing with the use of the strategic air force, to which we will return in our discussion of the planning of *Overlord*.

As regards the land forces, the two principal commanders were Generals Montgomery (British) and Bradley (American). No commander-in-chief was appointed for the land troops, which remained directly under Eisenhower. But for the actual assault, where limited forces would be committed on a narrow front, Montgomery was put in command of the two armies to be deployed, one Anglo-Canadian, the other American. At 56, Montgomery had a long career behind him as a soldier, during the First World War (when he won the D.S.O. [*Distinguished Service Order*] while very seriously wounded), in Palestine in 1936, commanding a division in France in 1939-1940, then in Africa and in Italy as commander of Eighth Army where he came to public attention. Full of energy and will-power, careful of his image, capable of being liked and esteemed in spite of his austere bearing, stiff and occasionally even individualistic, pious, making great demands on himself, with good tactical sense, very attentive to detail, he was a meticulous organiser. This last quality, a major contributory factor in his victories, made him an ideal choice for mounting the assault on the Normandy coast since any operation of this kind would require rigorous and precise planning, with so many actions affecting each other and following each other according to a precise timetable, and bringing a great number of units on different footings into play.

all of his own, firm and yet pleasant. He had a remarkable and very personal gift for turning miscellaneous commanders and formations into efficient combat units by exercising authority firmly and in a human and convincing manner. At 49 years of age, he was truly in his prime.

On arriving in London on 15 January 1944, he found British General Morgan, who had been directing the COSSAC staff for close on a year. He kept him on as deputy Chief of Staff. As Chief of Staff he placed the extremely efficient and precise General Bedell Smith who had been his Chief of Staff for *Torch* and the Mediterranean operations since September 1942. Until then mostly British, the Chiefs of Staff very soon saw more and more American officers and generals, in line with the growth and eventual predominance of the American forces.

The navy and air force commanders had already been appointed: for the navy, it was

**Army General
Omar N. Bradley,
Chief of the US 1st Army force
during D–Day operations
under Montgomery.**
(U.S.I.S. document)

The commander of U.S. First Army was General Bradley. At 51, he had 32 years of life as a soldier behind him; a stalwart infantryman, although not having had the opportunity to fight until 1942, he had nevertheless had long experience in command. He had served in the troops. For a long time he had been an instructor at West Point and at the infantry school, where he was in charge in 1941, during the period of rapid growth of the American army. He also served under General Marshall at that same school during the 1920s, then at General Staff in 1940. He had the total confidence of Generals Marshall and Eisenhower. Like the latter, he graduated from West Point in 1915 during the First World War in which neither of them were able to take any part. He rejoined Eisenhower in 1942 in North Africa as his deputy for special missions. He later commanded an army corps in Sicily. In command for the first time in battle, he immediately made his mark. The precision of his tactical sense, his straightforward judgement, his calm and assured demeanour and easy manner earned him the confidence of subordinates and superiors alike. Eisenhower intended him to take over the command of the American army group that would be constituted once the bridgehead had been widened enough to hold 4 armies in two - American and British - army groups.

The commander of Second Anglo-Canadian Army was to be General Dempsey (British) a veteran of the campaign in France, evacuated from Dunkirk in 1940, a former pupil of Montgomery's at the Staff College at Camberley, he was a reserved officer, very self-possessed, with little regard for publicity, and extremely competent. An infantryman, he had commanded a tank division. In 1940, he was attached to Canadian troops stationed in England. His familiarity with the Canadians and especially his former ties with Canadian corps commander General Simonds, would make his command easier, as would, later on, his connections with Canadian First Army when it came into being once the bridgehead had been widened.

Two other commanders deserve special mention: General F. W. de Guingand (British) had followed General Montgomery as Army Group Chief of Staff, and had long served under him. As a young officer, he had followed Major Montgomery's courses in tactics in New York in 1923. In 1931, he had been alongside Lieutenant-Colonel Montgomery commanding a battalion at Alexandria. Since 13 August 1942, the day General Montgomery took command in Libya, he was his Chief of Staff. He was a remarkable complement to his chief who had absolute confidence in him and left him plenty of room for initiative. Calm and capable, he smoothed over any occasional acerbity provoked by his commander and always managed to come to some agreement with Eisenhower and Bradley's Chiefs of Staff to find effective ways of executing orders that were sometimes difficult to reconcile.

One other commander, General Patton, was initially kept in reserve by Eisenhower. A 58-year-old tank cavalryman, like Montgomery a legendary figure, he was a courageous fighter. He took part in the Mexico campaign in 1917 and fought in France in 1918 where he was wounded at Argonne. He was a tank specialist. He commanded the American land forces that landed in Morocco on 8 November 1942, an army corps in Tunisia and an army in Sicily and Italy. He was known for his daring but always triumphant initiatives, but also for his unpredictable pranks and occasional outspokenness, notably with the press, who were merciless with him; but Eisenhower was banking on him to seize any opportunities to launch offensive operations and exploit them as quickly and as far as possible.

General Sir Miles Dempsey Chief of the British 2nd Army forces during D-Day operations.
(I.W.M. document)

The troops were equally varied, some hardened, others not. Among the hardened ones there were 4 American divisions and 3 British divisions that had come back from the Mediterranean in November 1943. There were also a great number of British officers and soldiers of the Home Forces, many of whom were among the 330,000 survivors of the expeditionary force to France in 1940, and after Dunkirk were readied to repulse the German invasion, and subsequently sent to fight overseas, whence a certain number returned.

Nearly all the American divisions, on the other hand, had been created in the course of 1941 and 1942. In July 1939 the American army and air force together totalled 130,000 men (including 17,000 airmen) on American soil and 45,000 overseas. By the end of 1939, this figure had risen to 227,000 men and, to 375,000 in June 1940.

With the mobilisation of the *National Guard* and the introduction of selective call-up, by autumn 1941 the numbers had reached 1,500,000 men. However it was only four months after Pearl Harbour, in the spring of 1942 that a law was passed authorising the general extension of national service and the dispatch of conscripts overseas. The American army of roughly 6 divisions (none armoured) in 1939, numbered over 100 in 1945. Initially organised into 4 armies in vast camps like Fort Benning or Fort Sam Houston, these divisions underwent intense and methodical training, took part in large-scale manoeuvres in the open countryside; thus in September 1941, the 270,000 men of Third Army, with Colonel Eisenhower as Chief of Staff, were opposed to the 130,000-strong Second Army in Louisiana. Simple tactical moves were developed, supporting fire, inter-army links, often characterised by their novelty and spirit of imagination, but also by their strict precision. As the land and air

General Crerar, appointed commander of the 1st Canadian Army at the beginning of August 1944.
(Canadian public archives)

These commanders all differed in their military training, experience, life-styles, their strategic and national ideas and their characters. But the war had brought them closer. Several had been working together for more than a year in the Mediterranean. They shared two common characteristics: their deep sense of human freedom stirred their cold, steadfast will to conquer. Also they were close to the men under them. Thus a British general paid the following fine tribute to General Eisenhower: "Eisenhower forgot himself entirely. Winning the war was the only thing that mattered to him; also, what was needed was a soldiers' general with deep concern for the men under him. It sometimes happens, unfortunately, that when those in command reach the top, they forget that it is men who win wars. However sophisticated all the available military hardware, it required men to handle the equipment. Eisenhower never forgot that, he always had a very deep feeling for the men under his command and, funnily enough, this got through very quickly to the troops engaged in the fighting." There would be many examples of this human feeling during the battle of Normandy.

forces were raised, the so-called "Bolero" plan was developed from spring 1942 to ship to Britain, initially to the north of Ireland, the divisions that were to carry out the operations in Europe. Some of these had been redirected to operation Torch in French North Africa, to be replaced by others arriving from America. This steady build-up meant that by the end of May 1944 nearly two million American women and men, airmen and land troops, had arrived on British soil.

In addition to the British and American forces, some Canadian divisions were also present. These were organised on British lines; some of them had taken part in the fighting in Africa; others had been in England for a long time and were well trained. Belgian, Polish, Irish, Norwegian and French contingents of various sizes and abilities were also to be found in England.

The cohabitation and training of all these formations were not problem-free in such a tiny, densely populated country, and so intensively cultivated, although still dependent on imports for a third of its subsistence, bombed and at war for 4 years. The British sense of organisation, American friendliness and the common will to win shown by all, whether Anglo-Americans or continental refugees, made any problems that occurred that much easier to solve. Whilst doubtless temperament and different customs as well as the practical difficulties of life caused occasional friction, it was always short-

lived. After 3 years of isolation, the British were comforted by the presence of friendly forces whom they welcomed with touching and familiar kindness. The Allied contingent readily consented to the discipline because they felt it imperative if their efforts towards final victory were not to be wasted. Friendly ties were created throughout the land. They eased relations between the two services, the American army - only newly raised and brought over, mostly with no combat experience, but with the benefit of the fervour of youth and the support of the most heavily industrialised country in the world -, and the British army - proud of its ancient traditions and recent hard battles -, receiving them as their host.

General Patton Jr chief of the American 3rd Army forces comprising General Leclerc's 2nd AD was involved in the Utah Beach landing on 31 July. His " blood & guts " reputation had gone before him.
(U.S.I.S. document)

Die Wehrmacht

HERAUSGEGEBEN VOM OBERKOMMANDO DER WEHRMACHT

8. Jahrgang · Nr. 10 · Berlin, 10. Mai 1944
Einzelpreis 25 Reichspfennig und Bestellgeld
Erscheint vierzehntäglich

„Vorstrand-Sperren" vor Hollands Küsten

Die Überflutung weiter Flächen hat Holland zu einer „Wasserfestung" gemacht. Den überfluteten und angesumpften Gebieten und den Dünen und Dämmen vorgelagert sind die ins Wasser hineinreichenden „Vorstrandsperren". Im Vordergrund ein Tobrukstand

(Vgl. unseren Bericht „Wasserfestung Holland" im Innern)

PK-Aufnahme
Kriegsberichter
Tritschler

INVASION DE L'EUROPE?

CHAPTER FIVE

THE GERMAN

DEFENCES

Left:
Atlantic wall defences make front page news in the magazine « Die Wehrmacht ».

Spring 1944, a German reconnaissance unit in the Pays d'Auge.
(E.C.P.A. document)

At the top of the military hierarchy stood Hitler. Often, since 1933, he had forced the hand of his generals with initiatives that his military commanders judged over-daring, and yet on which fortune had smiled. The remilitarisation of the left bank of the Rhine was the first in a long string of successes: the seizure of Austria and Czechoslovakia, fighting the war on two fronts, the dangers of which were eliminated with the lightning offensive in Poland, the defeat of France obtained thanks to a campaign plan modified at the suggestion of the FŸhrer himself, the Russian offensive. Convinced of his intuitive military genius, both strategic and tactical, and secure in the belief in the superiority of his ideas over the cautious pessimism of his generals, Hitler intervened directly at the level of the conduct of the war, but also at operational command level. He left no initiative to his generals, and, with rare exceptions, had little confidence in them: he controlled them through the commanders of the large S.S. units, who had received separate training and during operations were mixed in with the other army formations.

As long as Germany was on the offensive, until the start of 1943, Hitler found his generals to be remarkable tacticians capable of successfully exploiting his bold moves however rash they might be. Once he was thrown back on the defensive however, he made it his governing principle not to yield an inch of ground, thus gaining as much time as possible. He intended that any time gained in this manner would enable German industry, which by the end of 1943 was operating at maximum capacity, to produce his new secret weapons under the threat of which the Allies would be forced to seek terms. This principle of holding one's ground whatever the cost was put into practice in Russia, then in Tunisia and Italy, and left the German forces with no room to manoeuvre, and led them to fight futile and heroic battles to hold fixed defensive positions foot by foot, being gradually overwhelmed and surrounded, only to collapse in whole sections. Units remarkable for their tactical knowledge, their combat experience and courage were thus transformed into hordes of prisoners leaving countless dead on the ground behind them.

The well conceived plans for withdrawal put forward by the generals along shortened lines such as might have avoided these massacres were invariably rejected by Hitler.

In the west, Hitler had long been expecting a landing. Intelligence that came in after the Tehran conference confirmed the date as the spring of 1944. This was not unwelcome news to him.

The experience of the two previous years had taught him that he could not conquer the Soviet Union as long as he had to maintain a third of his army and a far greater proportion of his air force to face the threat of a second front.

On the other hand, once he had repulsed the cross-Channel invasion - as he had no doubt he would -, he would be able to concentrate his entire forces in order to obtain final victory in the east. He would hold the United Kingdom and United States on the defensive when his new weapons came into service - revolutionary submarines, jet-propelled aircraft, flying bombs, etc.

Although he was quite sure that he would repel the aggression, Hitler did not underestimate its importance. On 20 March, his three commanders-in-chief in the west, von Rundstedt (ground), Krancke (navy) and Sperrle (air), were summoned to Berchtesgaden to receive his instructions in connection with the landing now deemed certain:

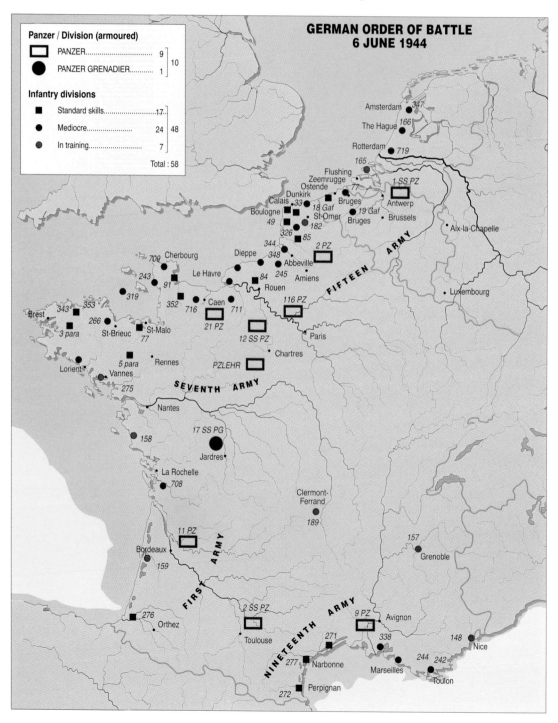

**Marshall von Rundsted
commander of the western
German forces on D-Day.
When the war was over
the author often asked
former German officers who,
in their opinion, had been
their best leaders. The top two
names were always:
− 1 von Rundstedt
− 2 von Manstein
Followed by a variety of names.
Rommel always came
way down the list.**
(E.C.P.A. document)

"The destruction of the attempted invasion is far more that an operation of local importance to the western front. It is the sole decisive factor in the conduct of the entire war and, consequently, in its final outcome."

Hitler developed his themes: "Any landing that has once failed will never be resumed. Besides the huge losses sustained, a new attempt would take months; and this would not be the only factor that would rule it out. The failure would cause an indelible moral shock. It would prevent the re-election of Roosevelt. In England, war weariness would reach a point never reached before. Due to his age, state of health, and his responsibility in the failure, Churchill would no longer be in a position to attempt a new landing." He concluded: "The fate of the war and the Reich is in the hands of each fighting man in the west."

Hitler had a clear view on how to face the assault: "The landing operation must not be allowed to develop for more than a few hours or days at the outside." It remained to find out "when" and "where" to expect the enemy. The answer to the first question depended on good weather reports. Unlike the Allies, Germany did not have numerous weather stations scattered across the globe, and therefore could not come up with a reliable long-term forecast. As for the place, Hitler correctly stated: "Whatever the concentration of shipping observed, it cannot be indicative of the choice made by the Anglo-Americans between Norway and the Bay of Biscay." Moreover Hitler was badly informed. The civil and military intelligence services, the latter being close to the party, were opposed and trying to outbid each other. Gradually overwhelmed by Anglo-American superiority, the air force was having growing difficulties in getting its spotter planes through. Those in charge of intelligence erred on the side of caution, tending to exaggerate the Allies' resources.

The commander-in-chief of the ground forces in the west since July 1942 was 69-year-old Marshal von Rundstedt. The eldest of the German officers, he represented the traditions of the old army to which he had belonged since the start of the century. In 1932, he held the most important command in the army, over Army Group 1 covering Berlin and Brandenburg: he witnessed the various movements that arose from political changes at the end of the Weimar republic on Hitler's rise to power, sometimes actually getting involved. As all officers of his generation and background that found themselves at the head of the small army that von Seekt had helped to survive, he accepted out of discipline, and with a certain contempt, the rise of Nazism, which at least had the merit of

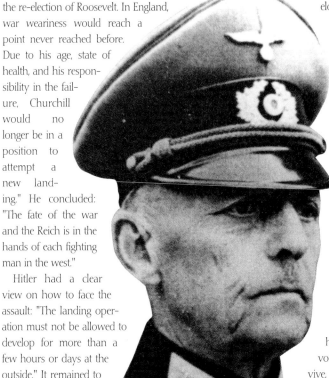

providing the army with weaponry, troops, modernisation and power. But he was one of those that Hitler's boldness had shaken and shocked. In 1938 his request for retirement on grounds of age was granted. A brilliant tactician, he was recalled to service in 1939: he achieved one victory after another commanding Army Groups in Poland in 1939, in France in 1940, and at the heart of the attack in Russia in 1941. When he fell into disagreement with Hitler over what should be done in Russia during the winter of 1941-l942, he retired again.

Unable to finish off Russia within a few months as anticipated, Hitler was obliged to consider the opening of a second front in the west and allocate about forty divisions to cover this eventuality. For this vital command, the ever victorious General von Rundstedt was recalled once again. A rather worn-out figurehead, subtle, and cultured, extremely polite, covered with honours, disillusioned, keeping his flickering flame alight on champagne, von Rundstedt set up his headquarters at Saint-Germain. He had little confidence in the "Atlantic wall" and in obstacles intended to halt the enemy. Sticking to the traditional tenet of mobility that had brought him success, he wanted to set up his reserves so as to throw back into the sea the disembarking forces, and was ready to hold back from attacking the enemy forces until they had landed in such numbers that being thrown back into the sea would signify their resounding and definitive defeat. Among possible landing zones, he gave priority to the Pas-de-Calais, discounting the Normandy coast on the grounds that it did not provide ready access to a port. Through the weakness of German intelligence, he was unaware that the year before Churchill had initiated the manufacture of elements enabling an artificial port to be built.

In the West, he had 50 divisions, and requested 70, and in June 1944 he had obtained around sixty. His command was over a combination of two Army Groups: "G "(von Blaskowitz) south of the Loire; "B" to the north including: LXXXVIII Corps in Holland, Fifteenth Army from Antwerp to the Orne, Seventh Army from the Orne to the Loire.

At the start of 1944, Hitler appointed to head Army Group "B" a commander in whom he placed his entire confidence, Rommel, the youngest marshal, putting him in charge of repulsing the Allied invasion that would certainly take place in his sector. Rommel's ideas, the fruit of his experience acquired in Libya, were different from those of his superior von Rundstedt. Allied air supremacy, which he had no doubt would be as massive as he had known it in Africa, would rule out any mobility among the reserves. The Allied assault had therefore to be repelled on the beaches themselves and no later than D-Day itself. All tank resources would have to be deployed near the coast so as to be able to act as quickly as possible. Similarly, the coastal defences, in which von Rundstedt had little faith, would play a vital role, and should be increased to reach maximum efficiency. On taking over command, Rommel was well aware of the situation, since in previous weeks, being available since his return from Africa, he had received a mission from Hitler to inspect and assess the defences in the face of a possible invasion from Norway to Spain.

He had come to the conclusion - once again in contradiction with von Rundstedt - that the most dangerous sector was the coast of Normandy. Nevertheless the defences had to be uniform

General von Blaskowitz, commander of the group G armies to the south of the Loire.
(F.C.P.A. document)

Rommel, as a young officer (left) during World War I. He was awarded a 2nd class Iron Cross in 1914, a 1st class Iron Cross at the beginning of 1915. Wounded twice, promoted to the rank of lieutenant in 1915, he took over as commander of a company in the Vosges, then served in Rumania, where he was wounded for a third time, followed by the Italian Alps.
(E.C.P.A. document)

Marshall Rommel commander of the group B armies from Holland to the Loire during D-day operations.
(R.H.A. document)

commanders of the calibre of von Rundstedt and Rommel, most of the Panzer Divisions could not be engaged without the Führer's personal consent. By virtue of the same vagaries of centralism, naval forces for coastal supervision, and Krancke and Sperrle's air forces in the west (350 planes), were not answerable to von Rundstedt, but directly responsible to the air and navy C-in-Cs, Dönitz and Goering.

This was even the case for the 88 mm anti-aircraft gun units - although they could be effective against tanks - and ground divisions of the Luftwaffe.

Rommel took over command on 15 January 1944, while on the other side of the Channel, the invasion command structure was also taking shape. Under Eisenhower, the ground force commander was to be none other than his old enemy in the desert, Montgomery.

because the Allied offensive would probably combine a main attack and a diversionary one. Intuitively, from May 1944, Hitler, who up till then had had the defensive effort carried out in the northern sector, like Rommel considered Normandy the more likely invasion zone.

Not only, however, did the two military commanders who would have the greatest part to play in the mission to repel the invasion have differing views on the matter, there was also the complexity of the command structure.

Von Rundstedt had under him a tank commander, Geyr von Schweppenburg, whose traditional ideas were similar to his own and who had learnt the lessons of the victorious campaign of 1939 to 1942. His role would be negligible in any case, since, by virtue of a principle of central command due to Hitler's mistrustfulness, even towards

Thus, at the same time, preparations were being stepped up on either side for the big showdown on which the fate of the war and the balance of the world depended.

Rommel set up his H.Q. at La Roche-Guyon, on the Seine near Vernon, in the castle at La Rochefoucauld, halfway between Paris and Le Havre, and not far from the shores that he was to defend. Having carried out his inspection mission as previously ordered by Hitler, he was well aware of the situation, both as regards the Atlantic wall fortifications and the troops entrusted to guard it.

The "Atlantic wall" referred, in theory, to concrete fortifications and secondary defences along the entire coastline of the North Sea, the English Channel and the Atlantic Ocean. What had been in 1940 offensive systems in the Pas-de-Calais became defensive after 1941 in order to protect the heart of Germany against any advance along the shortest route. Moreover launch pads for the V.-1 flying bombs were due for installation in this same area. For this reason the defensive construction work here had gone ahead more quickly, and there were more and bigger defence works.

Elsewhere, organisation had lacked conviction. This was partly due to von Rundstedt's scepticism, but this was only one of many reasons: lack of cooperation and even sabotage by French workers employed by the "Todt" organisation; shortage of materials owing to bombing raids on factories and on communications channels disrupting supplies; French resistance operations against convoys and railways; and lastly the German shortage of troops.

In the west since 1941 were stationed exhausted, undermanned units that had been brought back from Russia to rest and recuperate, and were consequently not eager for the work that they were given to adapt the terrain in order to complete the fortifications.

Rommel set to work with his usual energy as he had done throughout his career, whether as an eager young officer during the First World War, as commander of 7th Panzer in 1940, or in Tripoli in charge of the Afrikakorps. He immediately gave it everything he had in both mental and physical terms. Constantly on the move, he would go in person to accelerate construction projects, put all army units to work, and devised new obstacles. Convinced that the landing would take place at high tide so as to carry troops and vehicles as near as possible to the active defences and objectives, he crammed the beaches with obstacles of his own invention to rip open landing-craft and vehicles, and immobilise the infantry under gunfire from automatic weapons and coastal batteries: crossed iron stakes, pointed rails stuck in the ground, concrete tetrahedra, mines in the sea and on the beaches, hedgehogs and concrete levees intended to block beach exits for the tanks.

Germany occupation propaganda.
(« Notre combat », January 1944)

He had the low lands flooded (southwest of Carentan for example) and had open terrain suitable for parachute drops and glider landings covered with "Rommel's asparagus" (sharp stakes pointed upwards). He extended his efforts to all parts of the coast, regardless of his personal opinion as to the likelihood of the landing occurring there. And there was all the less room for sloppiness in the Pas-de-Calais, where the launch sites were being built for Hitler's secret weapons, the V.- l, now in production.

The German navy had a new and very efficient type of underwater mine; however, owing to inadequate production and especially lack of coordination between the navy and army commands, they were not laid in advance but were not to be used until the time of the landing itself, which, of course, could not be done properly.

Further inland, between the fortress of Cherbourg and Caen, a dozen fortified underground batteries, such as those at Saint-Marcouf, at the base of the Cotentin, and Merville, near the mouth of the Orne, covered the beaches with their gunfire, and could even reach shipping out to sea.

At the time of the landing, the German defences had been considerably improved in the course of the last four months, largely thanks to Rommel: obstacles were set up and units were trained. There were however gaps due to the deficiency of some units, insufficient intelligence, poor organisation at command level, particularly as regards use of tanks.

The quality of the German divisions in the West (48 + 10 armoured) was uneven: some were excellent, well trained and well equipped, others were made up of very young recruits, with inadequate instruction, others came from the east and were reformed with experienced but tired soldiers; others comprised mostly foreigners whose performance was unpredictable. There were also shortages due to equipment, guns and ammunition not arriving, not so

much through faulty manufacturing processes as just not getting through: thus at the time of the landing, pillboxes sometimes lacked the guns that they had been built to use. The disparity, or maybe even rivalry between the army units and S.S. formations was to complicate human relations in a chain of command that the centralisation imposed by Hitler made slow and ponderous.

Von Rundstedt and Rommel's knowledge of the enemy was poor. The German air force was having more and more trouble with reconnaissance. The few spies sent to England had nearly all been discovered and arrested. Rivalry between the army intelligence service and the civilian service close to the party led them to vie with each other in their valuations of the Allied forces: thus, at the end of July 1944, nearly two months after the landing, while the Normandy pocket had been stretched to such an extent as no longer left any doubt as to its importance (almost 30 divisions), the German intelligence services indicated the existence on British soil of close on 40 American divisions waiting to launch a second assault in Picardy. This had implied the presence in England at the beginning of June of at least double the number of divisions there actually had been. True, this error of judgment was fostered by an Allied "deception plan", an integral part of the preparation which continued throughout the unfolding of Overlord.

Under Rommel, Army Group B command structure was as follows:

- LXXXVIII Corps Holland: 4 divisions;
- Fifteenth Army (von Salmuth) from Antwerp to the Orne: 17 divisions;
- Seventh Army (Dollmann) from the Orne to Saint-Nazaire: 14 divisions.

Army Group G (south of the Loire) numbered 13 divisions, 4 facing the Atlantic, 7 facing the Mediterranean, 2 under instruction in the centre of France.

The mobile armoured reserve comprised 10 divisions (5 S.S., 5 army) 6 of which were stationed north and 4 south of the Loire. They were all administratively controlled by Panzer Group West under General Geyr von Schweppenburg. But for operational work, it was different. 3 had been assigned to Rommel for tactical deployment:

- 2lst Panzerdivision (General Feuchtinger), near Caen;
- 116th Panzer (General von Schwerin), this fomer Afrikakorps division had been reformed north of Mantes;
- 2nd Panzer (General von Luttwitz), near Abbeville.

The 3 other divisions stationed north of the Loire together made up 1st S.S. Panzerkorps, under the command of Obergruppenführer S.S. Sepp Dietrich:

- Panzerlehrdivision (General Bayerlein), a socalled training division which was in fact a new

Front page of the magazine of the German army (" Die Wehrmacht ") in July 1944 featuring Field Marshall Rommel in Normandy.

130 armoured Panzer–Lehr regiment reaching Juaye–Mondaye, approximately 4 miles from Bayeux on 8 June 1944.
(E.C.P.A. document)

experimental division, with a powerful tank force, east of Le Mans;

– 12th S.S. "Hitler Youth" Panzer Division (S.S. Obergruppenführer Witt), near Evreux;

– lst S.S. "Leibstandart" Panzer Division (S.S. Obergruppenführer Wisch), near Antwerp.

These 3 divisions as well as 17th S.S. Panzer-grenadierdivision (Poitiers) were kept in strategic reserve by von Rundstedt, but could not be committed without explicit permission from the German High Command (Ober Kommando der Wehrmacht [O.K.W.]), basically, in other words, Hitler himself.

This division of the command imposed by Hitler prevented the command in the West – and hence Rommel – from using the reserves, and left division commanders uncertain as to

which he organically belonged. On the other hand, he knew that he could not move without orders from Rommel of Army Group B. As for the other divisions, they could not move without orders from Hitler himself.

This arrangement did not satisfy Rommel. Applying his own idea to fight the battle on the beaches themselves as soon as the invasion had started, he had brought his infantry divisions up close to the coast. Hence the Allies' surprise on 6 June to find right on Omaha beach the excellent 352nd Division that had just been brought in to flank the indifferent 7l6th.

Likewise, Rommel wanted to place his tank reserves up on the coast, but he came up against von Rundstedt, Geyr von Schweppenburg, and even tank commander-in-chief

Panzer IV of the 12th S.S. "Hitler Youth " regiment pictured at Mailly–le–Camp in April 1944.
(E.C.P.A. document)

who they were responsible to in the event of any intervention. Thus General Feuchtinger, commanding 2lst Panzer, closest to the Normandy coast, did not know in the event of invasion – and still did not know on 6 June – whether he was to act to orders of 711th Division (Fifteenth Army - east of the Orne), 7l6th Division (Seventh Army - west of the Orne) within which he was stationed or Panzer Group West (Geyr von Schweppenburg) to

Guderian. Hitler had settled the matter by deciding on a middle course which gave him 3 Panzer divisions, a compromise decision that satisfied nobody. It was for this very purpose - to plead in favour of a different solution and to obtain at least one extra Panzer division, that on 5 June Rommel decided to go and see Hitler, and was absent from his H.Q. during the landing on the 6th, which further complicated the situation and delayed decision-making.

Allied chiefs of staff: seated from left to right: Tedder, Eisenhower, Montgomery: Standing from left to right: Bradley, Ramsay, Leigh-Mallory, Bedell-Smith.

(I.W.M. document)

CHAPTER SIX

OVERLORD STRATEGY TAKEN OVER BY EISENHOWER

(JANUARY 1944)

Eisenhower's insignia. Emblem of the Supreme Headquarters Allied Expeditionary Forces. The sword symbolises the combined allied forces joined in the fight against Nazism. The black represent darkness for obscurity with the rainbow of liberty breaking over it.

General Eisenhower, appointed Supreme Commander Allied Expeditionary Force (S.C.A.E.F.), in charge of the invasion operation against the mainland of Europe, returned to London on 15 January, where he set up his H.Q. (Supreme Headquarters Allied Expeditionary Force [S.H.A.E.F.]).

The situation awaiting Eisenhower resulted, in general terms, from decisions taken by the Allied Chiefs of Staff Committee (C.C.S.), since its inception in January 1942 and, more immediately, from research and operations undertaken by General Morgan (COSSAC) since March 1943.

The favourable turn taken by the battle of the Atlantic in June 1943 had made it possible to send and build up American forces in Great Britain.

The plans required an army of 1,446,000 men to be raised by the spring of 1944. At the end of 1943, the figure had reached almost a million. In November 1943, 7 divisions including 4 American were brought back from Italy to England so as to have units with combat experience alongside recently formed units sent over from America.

Attacks by the strategic air forces (British Bomber Command and the American Strategic Air Force) against the German war machine were carried out in accordance with decisions taken at the Casablanca conference in January 1943, and intensified from June 1943. Directly coordinated by C.C.S., their object was 6 vulnerable industrial groups over which the Germans were particularly sensitive: submarines, ball-bearings, rubber, aircraft manufacture, fuel and communications. These last 3 were a constant priority. During 1943 the arrival in England of American long-range fighters capable of escorting bombers right up to their targets made it possible henceforward to deal effective blows against industrial centres set in the very heart of Germany. American air forces on English soil numbered over a thousand aircraft.

Material for the invasion was being gathered in England. Some of it was currently in the Mediterranean and would be redirected to the Channel after the projected landing in late January at Anzio near Rome, behind the German lines on the Garigliano. COSSAC had demonstrated the inadequacy of available resources, particularly in L.S.T.s (Landing Ship Tanks) capable of landing 80 vehicles, including 25 tanks, and 350 men.

COSSAC had devised a plan for the amphibious assault, its consolidation and the manoeuvre on land immediately following. He had collected vast quantities of information about the coast, beaches and the German defences.

Special equipment, amphibious tanks, amphibious vehicles, elements for the artificial ports, already existed or were in the process of manufacture. They were the fruit of the research and imagination of the Combined Operations Command under Mountbatten. Some had been experimented, as had the various landing craft, Landing Ships, both in the Pacific and in the Mediterranean by order of Eisenhower himself.

Eisenhower's immediate preoccupations would be:

- the organisation of the command structure;
- the strategic philosophy;
- the amphibious assault plan, taking German defences into account;

– preparations in the air;
– the plan for the manoeuvre on land;
– the training of troops.

These various tasks would occupy Eisenhower, his subordinates and his headquarters in the course of the coming 4 months between the general's arrival and the landing itself, planned to take place immediately after 1st May.

On taking command, Eisenhower found a staff already up and running, having been operational since April 1943 under COSSAC, the British General Morgan. He appointed as its head General Bedell Smith (U.S.), who had occupied the same position at his side in the Mediterranean. He gave him as second-in-command General Morgan, who had prepared the plans approved in Quebec in August 1943, and who had since introduced measures which would take a long time to implement, notably gathering intelligence and organising deception. This staff was considerably strengthened with personnel from the United States, and numbered no less than 750 officers and 6,000 men. Based to the west of London, its task was to set in train a main striking force the vastness of which was on a scale unique in military history, as a few figures at H-Hour would demonstrate with no need for further comment.

Eisenhower and Montgomery had lived through 1943 on the Mediterranean theatre. At

the time of their appointment in December, they knew nothing of the plans prepared by COSSAC and approved in Quebec in August. In late December at Marrakech in Morocco, they both met Churchill who was recovering after the Tehran conference from ill-health resulting from his inexhaustible energy and the weight of responsibility he had borne without interruption since 1939. Informed by Churchill of the COSSAC plan, both agreed with Churchill's position in Quebec, namely that it lacked size and scope and thus entailed excessive risk.

On leaving Marrakech for Washington, Eisenhower ordered Montgomery, who reached London on 2 January 1944, to work with Ramsay, Leigh-Mallory and Bedell Smith on a possible revision of the COSSAC plan towards widening the amphibious assault front so as to enable Cherbourg to be captured quickly, and which would require greater resources that needed to be quantified as quickly as possible. With characteristic meticulousness and sense of organisation, Montgomery set to work straight away on arriving in London, and put his staff to work.

When the plan was originally thought out, COSSAC had been limited by the quantity of air and sea resources, particularly in specialised landing ships, approximately 3,000 *Landing Ships* and landing craft of all types allocated to him by C.C.S.

On the one hand, C.C.S. was torn between the requirements of the various theatres in the Pacific, Indian Ocean and Burma, the Mediterranean and the English Channel. On the other hand, estimations of landing craft capacities had been considerably higher than was actually the case.

Since any operational landing has to be effected rapidly under gunfire on open beaches, this requires vehicles to be spaced, which reduces the nominal capacity of a given vessel by at least a tenth, sometimes more, compared with the transportation over long distances, say across the Pacific, of tanks or combat vehicles.

The absence of a commander-in-chief designate had prevented COSSAC from putting forward his views with sufficient weight on the risks involved in a skimped operation and getting them approved. The needs of Neptune, code-name of the seaborne portion of *Overlord*,

R.A.F. Bomber Command pilot posing for the camera in front of his "Stirling".
(I.W.M. document)

i.e. the amphibious assault and naval support, were competing with operations already under way in the Pacific. Churchill's comment in Quebec calling for a 25% increase in resources to be allocated to *Overlord* had only been wishful thinking with no concrete follow-up. The decision taken at Tehran in November 1943 to make the Overlord cross-Channel invasion - combined with a secondary landing in Provence (Anvil) and the resumption of the Soviet offensive in the east in the spring -, the dominating operation in 1944 changed the standpoint from which the respective needs of the various theatres had to be considered. Presumably during his visit to Washington early in January 1944, Eisenhower did not fail to prepare the various people he would be addressing to receive his request for a large increase in his allocated resources so as to carry through successfully the extended operation that in the meantime he had ordered Montgomery to research.

The COSSAC plan catered for an assault on a 25 mile long front, led by an army corps of 3 divisions with, hard on their heels, 3 follow-up corps of 3 to 4 divisions each, and flanked by 2 airborne assaults equivalent to 1 to 2 divisions.

In total, Montgomery promptly pointed out, by D + 12 (D for *Day* was the day of the 1st air- or seaborne landing on French soil) twelve divisions and their reinforcements would have come ashore on the same beaches used for the initial assault. This would lead to appalling confusion on the beaches and no end of difficulty in widening the beachhead. The initial assault therefore had to be launched on as broad a front as possible, each of the American and British armies coming in 2 or 3 corps abreast.

The first fortnight of January 1944 was devoted to studying ways of widening the assault zone so as to include beaches to the east as far as the mouth of the Orne, and to the west, those situated on the south-east coast of the Cotentin, with the advantage here of shortening

**" Landing Craft Assault ".
10 000 L.C.A. s were built in the
USA between 1943 and 1944.**
(R.H.A. document)

the distance to be covered in order to reach Cherbourg. The presence of marshy terrain, which Rommel had flooded, near Carentan, in the corner of the Cotentin peninsula on the lower Normandy side, made it imperative to drop an airborne force of around 2 divisions at the base of the Cotentin, the only possible way to join hands with separate amphibious assault forces on the other side of the marshland and capture Cherbourg quickly. Likewise in the east, on the Orne and beyond, an airborne force of at least a division was required on the eastern flank to cover the advance towards Caen. Given that, subsequently, one day in four might turn out unfavourable due to poor weather, it was to be hoped that sufficient resources could be brought ashore to cope with a German tank concentration expected from D + 4, and to reach a line Mont St. Michel-Alençon-Trouville by D + 14.

Such an extension involved:
– an airborne assault by 3 divisions (and not just one to one and a half as originally planned),
– an amphibious assault by 5 divisions (instead of 3),
– a corresponding increase in specialist techniques (beach engineers, etc.),
– the constitution of an "immediate follow-up" to the amphibious assault by 2 divisions, also to be pre-loaded onto landing-craft.

The breadth of the assault zone could thus be increased from 25 miles to nearly 50 miles. Such a modification involved an average 40% increase in amphibious vehicles and 20% in airborne requirements. Owing to the extension of the beaches to be pounded with shellfire, naval support had to be increased by an extra combat group, or *Task Force*.

Republic P.–47 fighter planes & B.–17 bombers lined up on an airfield in England ready for delivery to the units who were to fly over the continent.
(R.H.A. document)

**Air Marshal Leigh-Mallory,
Chief of the Allied Expedi-
tionary Air Forces.**
(I.W.M. document)

Faced with this extension of the airborne operation, which had practically been doubled, Leigh-Mallory objected that flak and difficult terrain at the base of the Cherbourg peninsula could result in 75% losses among forces engaged the western airborne operation.

The basic difficulty lay in the need to find around 1,000 extra landing-craft, when even the 3,200 already spoken for in the COSSAC plan were not yet definitely going to be available.

Immediately on arriving, on 15 January, Eisenhower examined this new plan put forward on 21 January. He approved and adopted it as a basis for Overlord preparations. But the execution of this plan could not be envisaged without deferring the provisional date of 1 May, owing to the non-availability of ships in sufficient numbers by that time. Postponing for a month would have the disadvantage of decreasing by as much the available time to launch the follow-up phase in the direction of Germany before winter set in. It might also upset Stalin who was expecting by 1st May the opening of the second front he had been urging for so long, having committed himself in Tehran to time the launching of his own offensive in the east to coincide with Overlord. On the other hand, whilst it was quite out of the question to dispose of landing equipment currently scattered across the Pacific, any such delay would make available an extra month's output from the

shipyards, whose activity had been intensified along the Atlantic coast of America since the end of 1943, particularly as regards L.S.T. (Landing Ship Tanks, carrying 350 men and 80 vehicles or tanks) whose role, and consequently any shortage, were crucial for the landing. Incidentally, the same went for the various special landing equipment, with production proceeding briskly.

Postponement would also present other advantages.

The reduction of German industrial potential by the Allied strategic air forces would benefit from an extra month in weather conditions that promised to be favourable; the extra time could be used to good effect since, as we have seen, in spite of the bombing campaign, Speer's energy had taken German industrial output to an all-time high in 1943.

Moreover, Eisenhower was considering stepping up strategic bombing operations against communication channels, in order to prevent Hitler from moving his forces, particularly his tank reserves, up to threatened areas.

A larger number of units, at least 2 divisions, reinforced with the necessary specialist staff, beach sappers, mine-sweepers, etc., had to be trained in preparation for the amphibious assault. It would be useful to have an extra month to train these people.

Furthermore, as we know, it was planned that another landing should be launched in conjunction with *Overlord*, the purpose of this second landing, code-named *Anvil*, on the coast of Provence, being to pin down the German forces and prevent them from being transferred to northern France or eastern Europe. Leaving a time interval between the two operations meant that the same landing craft could be used first in *Overlord* and then in the *Anvil* landing in Provence.

Eisenhower proposed to postpone *Overlord* for a month, and to delay Anvil until the end of July. He requested extra resources for the invasion, to be reinforced for extra safety and support by a naval combat group or *Task Force*. These various proposals and requests eventually obtained the assent of Roosevelt and Churchill, as well as the C.C.S. On 1st February it was finally decided to postpone *Overlord* for a month, with a new date set for early June; in late March, for there was a long

Aftermath of allied bombing raids on arsenal blockhouses.
(E.C.P.A. document)

debate with and within the C.C.S., *Anvil* was definitely deferred until the end of July; in mid-April it was decided to set up a American *Task Force* of 40 warships around 3 battleships for the benefit of *Overlord*.

These measures made available the necessary landing resources (6,047 *landing craft*) for the size of the assault forces recommended in the revised plan, namely:

– 176,500 men and 20,000 vehicles (including 3,000 guns, 1,500 tanks and 5,000 armoured vehicles) to be brought ashore in the first 48 hours of the invasion.

Without waiting for his proposals to be approved and his request accepted, Eisenhower pushed through very actively - in a real race against time - the planning of the operation, the production of equipment depending on his sole authority, and the training of men, units and Chiefs of Staff. By *D-Day*, Eisenhower was in command of a force the like of which had never been seen:

– 37 divisions on English soil, which, once they had disembarked, would be joined by 50 divisions arriving directly from the United States;

– a war fleet (battleships, monitors, cruisers and destroyers) comprising as many as 200 units with an additional fighting flotilla containing 500 boats

of different kinds (frigates, corvettes, patrol boats, minesweepers, torpedo boats, etc.);

– a supporting air fighter fleet of 171 flights (3,100 planes) not including strategic bombers depending on C.C.S., but which would be frequently used for the direct benefit of the forces engaged.

On 1st February, when the date of the landing was finalised, General Eisenhower had another 4 months to take the measures that would lead this huge striking force still being assembled to accomplish a mission on which the fate of the world depended, and the text of which did not reach him until 14 February.

The month of January 1944, just finished, marks the strategic takeover of *Overlord* by Eisenhower. Ever since July 1940, a return to the continent had been Churchill's ultimate objective. From January 1941, Roosevelt had become convinced that it would be necessary first of all to bring down Hitler's Germany in order to re-establish the world balance of power. Since July 1941, Stalin had been calling for the opening of the second front which alone would free the Soviet Union from the German threat.

This convergence of views had found expression in various efforts, which were coordinated, although sometimes in roundabout ways or using divergent methods; by often sharp controversies between the Allies as to ways and means; by painful renunciations; but also by research, weapons manufacture, the build-up, particularly in the United States, and effective preliminary operations.

The decision to widen the field of action and the initial resources finally opened a door that was big enough for the manoeuvre that would surge through it to reach Germany.

Eisenhower immediately had pushed through decisions for preparation and execution at the strategic objective level. Of course the decision-making process was not yet over. But even now he gave orders as if his proposals had already been accepted. It will be remembered that it was he who, early in 1942, took part in the preparation of contingency plans against a possible invasion of Europe, in the event of the Soviet Union being on the point of giving way under Hitler's attacks;

in July 1942, placed at the head of the American forces in Europe, he was the first to realise that the conditions for a successful invasion of Europe had not yet been achieved and that it was therefore preferable to drop that idea for a while and to land in North Africa; he held commands of increasing importance in North Africa, Sicily and Italy.

It took all the force of his kind and reasoned obduracy to convince the supreme authorities of the correctness of his position and to weld together the men placed under him in preparation for their mission. His assets were his experience, his even temper, his conscience, and the confidence that he brought to the task in hand and aroused in others.

The directive issued by the *Combined Chiefs of Staff* for *Overlord* is appended to this chapter: it did not reach London until mid-February. Eisenhower knew most of its contents on taking up his command.

L.C.T.s (" Landing Craft Tanks ") moored at an English port prior to the landing on 6 June 1944.
(R.H.A. document)

President Roosevelt with British Prime Minister W. Churchill at the Quadrant conference held in Quebec (17–24 August 1943). This conference was to ratify the "Overlord" plan prepared by C.O.S.S.A.C.. General Morgan (C.O.S.S.A.C.) was instructed to continue preparations and take the measures necessary for its execution during 1944 (special intelligence work, diversionary tactics, etc.). The French resistance, on which he had counted heavily for intelligence gathering, was being systematically wiped out during the same period.

(E.C.P.A. document)

CHAPTER SEVEN

THE PHILOSOPHY
OF THE MANOEUVRE

In any offensive operation, the philosophy of the manoeuvre is the operational - somewhat tactical - expression of the strategy that determines the military and political objective; it directs all decisions, including the initial assault. In the case of an amphibious assault, it involves considerable constraints for the course of the manoeuvre for which it opens the way: this is why the assault has a major place in the philosophy itself, as indeed was the case with *Overlord*.

Moreover, it was the preparation of the actual re-entry into Europe that had preoccupied Churchill for the last 4 years: he could never forget the painful Dardanelles episode during the First World War. Fortified by this experience, as early as 1940 he set to work not only on plans for combined operations, but also research and development of equipment for the amphibious phase of *Overlord*.

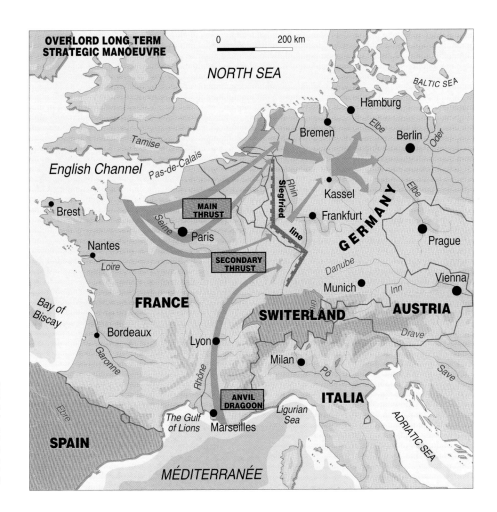

General Eisenhower's mission: " You shall penetrate the European continent, where, together with the other allied nations, you shall undertake operations to strike at the heart of German designed to destroy its armed forces..." (C.C.S., 12 February 1944.)

The directive received by Eisenhower on 15 February was the fruit of lengthy work based on the first plans drafted in Washington from December 1941 on. It was not impossible to recognise the handiwork of one of the planning officers, Lieutenant-Colonel (now General) Wedemeyer, former student at the German Kriegsakademie where he came into contact with the theories of the geopolitician Haushofer on the continental centre of power.

The long-term strategic philosophy behind the operation - the opening phase of which was the amphibious assault - was very briefly defined, in no more than a necessary and sufficient manner, because on it depended the whole succession of actions to be carried out starting on the beaches and going right up to the final defeat of Germany, and consequently the logistical preparation to be commenced without delay. The object was the very heart of Germany and the defeat of her armed forces. Now the heart of Germany, the centre of her power, was in the Ruhr. The German army could be destroyed, either before the Rhine and the Siegfried line, or, failing that, in Germany itself, at the same time that the Ruhr was reached. The strategic philosophy may be formulated as follows:

– land in Normandy (the choice of the landing place had already been made),

– build up power necessary resources for a decisive battle in the Normandy-Brittany area, and break through enemy positions surrounding the pocket,

– pursue on a broad front across France, by making efforts in the west to seize the ports; reach the German frontier and threaten the Ruhr; join hands with the forces coming from the south,

– while continuing the build-up of forces out of the ports in preparation for the final showdown, to lead the offensive with no let up, using maximum resources,

– destroy forces west of the Rhine, while seeking to cross that river,

– launch a final attack forming a double opening up of the Ruhr, with the main effort on the left flank. Break out across Germany in a direction yet to be defined, and clean up the rest of Germany.

The first points to emerge from this operational description are logistic concerns.

After the assault, the effort westward to secure the use of Cherbourg and the ports of Brittany; after the breakout, the effort eastward along the Channel to conquer in succession the ports of Le Havre, Antwerp and Rotterdam.

This way the men and equipment needed to carry the final blow to the heart of Germany, and primarily the Ruhr, could be shipped across into Europe.

Until this stage was reached, the prime concern was the amphibious assault, operation Neptune. Thus Eisenhower's first reaction on receiving his command in Africa was to ask Montgomery to study, revise and broaden the tactical conception of this initial operation. Similarly, the first decisions he made on arriving in London also involved this same operation.

The invasion plan was adopted but broadened, and appropriate resources immediately requested.

The command structure was set up quickly, in order that the commanders and troops concerned might prepare and train, and that staff dividing them into units adapted for shipping might begin their tedious and meticulous work without delay. In his operations memorandum, Eisenhower set out with great simplicity the objective and structure.

The plan of the invasion comprised an assault against beaches situated between Ouistreham and Varreville along a front five divisions wide, with the immediate aim of establishing beachheads for the follow-up troops coming in behind.

The initial object of the attack was the capture of Caen, Bayeux, Isigny and Carentan, as well as airfields situated in the vicinity of Caen, and also the vital port of Cherbourg. This done, our forces were to advance on Brittany in order to capture any ports as far as Nantes. Having achieved this, they would advance eastwards in the general direction of Paris and to the north, and crossing the Seine with a view to destroying the greatest possible number of German troops in this western sector.

As it had been planned later on to replenish the American forces with troops shipped directly from ports in the United States, the Americans were positioned on the righthand flank. It would be their job to seize Cherbourg and the ports of Brittany, whilst the British to the north and east were to capture the Channel ports as far as Antwerp so as to receive supplies directly from England. The entire

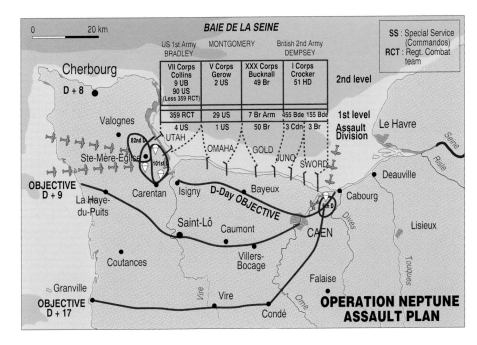

Plan illustrates:
– tactics of amphibious assaults,
– objectives set on the
following days:
• evening of D–Day,
• on D + 9
(including Cherbourg),
• on D + 17: Granville, Vire,
Condé, the area around Caen
(with its airfields and its
openings to the south–east).

organisation of the assault would be derived from these logistical considerations.

The U.S. First Army (Bradley) would attack the beaches at Varreville (code-named Utah) and Saint-Laurent (Omaha).

U.S. VII Corps (General Collins) would come ashore with 4th Infantry at Utah north of the mouth of the Vire. During the first hours of daylight, 82nd (General Gavin) and 101st (General Taylor) Airborne would drop in the zone south-east and west of Sainte-Mère-Eglise and seize bridges over the Merderet, thus securing the line of the Douve, so as to facilitate the landing of 4th Infantry, and link up with them.

V Corps (General Gerow) would attack the 3 1/2 mile wide Omaha beach, on the north coast of the Calvados, with infantry groupings (Combat Command) of U.S. 29th and 1st Infantry (under orders from the latter).

VII Corps' main objective was to cut the Cotentin peninsula in two, then to seize Cherbourg by D + 8. V Corps would push south towards Saint-Lô and hold it, if possible by D + 9.

The soldiers of British Second Army (General Dempsey) would land on 3 sectors of beach from Asnelles (Gold), the objective of the British 50th Division reinforced with elements of British 7th Armoured, Courseulles (Juno), the objective of the Canadian 3rd Division, and Ouistreham

(Sword), objective of the British 3rd Division; the first of these divisions was under orders from British III Corps (General Bucknall) and the two others from British 1st Corps (General Crocker). British 6th Airborne Division would be dropped behind the beach defences and west of the Orne, the river that flows through Caen, in order to secure the bridges over the Orne and the canal linking Caen and the sea.

These forces' brief was to seize, as quickly as possible, and if possible on D-Day, Caen and the open area and airfields that lay close to the town. The British forces' overall mission was to protect the left flank of the landing zone against German counter-attack, especially tank attacks, likely to come from the east, then to deploy as far as Vire-Falaise, to be reached by D + 20, so as to have a firm grip on the road network around Caen.

The advance was then projected to continue eastwards and northwards for the desired purpose of reaching the Seine from Le Havre to Paris, the gap from Paris to Orleans, and the Loire from Orleans to Nantes by D + 90.

Such was the overall scheme of things on the basis of which over a 3 month period Montgomery would gradually work out his detailed plan, gradually completed, modified, adjusted and fine-tuned.

" Ducks ", G.M.C. amphibious vehicles at the assembly point on the south coast of England.

(I.W.M. document)

CHAPTER EIGHT

PREPARATIONS

FOR THE ACTUAL ASSAULT
Timing and equipment used for the landing

After the place, the timing of the landing was a decision of the utmost importance. Several factors came into play.

In the Mediterranean, most combat landings had taken place under cover of darkness. For Neptune, the 3 commanders-in-chief and Eisenhower agreed to attack by day so as to facilitate the identification of the beaches, the navigation of the huge numbers of small craft, and observation of targets for air and naval bombardment. Ramsay and Leigh-Mallory wished to

dispose of a hour of daylight after dawn in order to shell the German defences; but this hour of daylight left the troops that had come ashore that much less time to widen the beachhead before nightfall; it might help the Germans to spot the approaching Allied armada and cause problems for a second wave of forces coming in the same day on the next tide.

The times of the tides were indeed an important factor. Anticipating a landing at dawn and at high tide, the Germans, through the impetus

Operation " Neptune ".

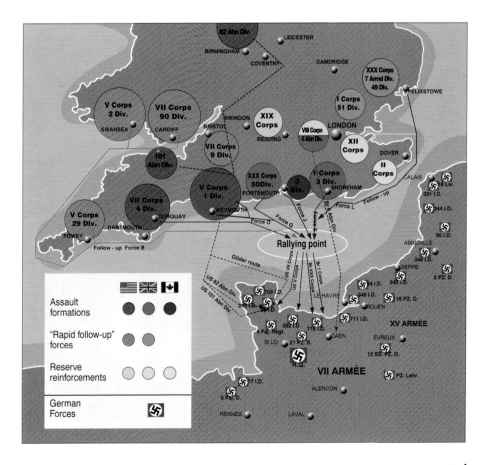

The Normandy coast prior to the landing. The obstacles laid by the Germans are uncovered by the low tide.
(E.C.P.A. document)

given by Rommel, had covered the beaches with invisible underwater obstacles which landing-craft and amphibious vehicles were to impale themselves on.

The Allies therefore decided to thwart German expectations and to land at low water or half-tide so as to be able to see the obstacles. On the other hand, high tide was earlier on *Utah beach* in the west (Varreville) than on the easternmost beach at *Sword* (Ouistreham).

Another consideration to be taken into account was the moon; a full moon late at night would facilitate the task of the airborne divisions approaching their targets from the air and due to jump several hours before the amphibious assault.

It was therefore ultimately decided that the assault would take place on a day when it would be half-tide on the westernmost beach (*Utah*) 40 minutes after first light, following a night when a full moon rose at between 1 and 2 a.m. There are 3 such days in any month; in June 1944, these were the 5, 6 and 7.

Additional considerations such as wind speed, visibility (cloud and fog) and hygrometry (density and frequency of rainfall) were analysed from past records, and contemporary weather forecasts.

Finally, on 17 May, 2 days after Montgomery had presented a complete exposition of the invasion plan, Eisenhower fixed D-Day for 5 June, with alternative dates on 6 and 7 June, depending on last-minute weather forecasts.

One important problem with an amphibious assault is that right from the start, even before touching dry land, the attacker meets organised resistance and heavy gunfire. All information obtained by Allied spotter planes or through the French resistance confirmed that under Rommel's command, both the active and passive German defences had been reinforced, especially in Normandy where they had previously been neglected. The supporting air and naval fire was intended to neutralise in advance the German defensive system until the very last moment. But initial contact with French soil would still be difficult and full of unforeseen hazards for the chests and feet of the Allied infantrymen.

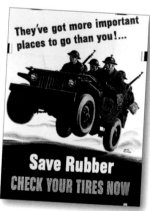

They've got more important places to go than you!...

Save Rubber
CHECK YOUR TIRES NOW

Propaganda poster.

Member of a British tank team.
(I.W.M. document)

Fortunately, for months past, special equipment had been designed to accompany and help the troops in their first approach to the beaches and German resistance.

Since March 1943, General Hobart's British 79th Armoured Division had conducted experiments intended to provide the infantry with immediate tank support without which the assault might have involved unbearable losses. The following were produced:
– bulldozer tanks designed to clear beach obstacles,
– "flail" tanks with projecting chains or metal blades used for mine-sweeping,
– tanks that fired explosive charges to blow up pillboxes and secondary defences,
– tanks carrying bridging elements to get across craters and ditches,
– flame-throwing tanks,
– also amphibious tanks known as D.D. (Duplex Drive) tanks.

The D.D. tank was capable of reaching land under its own steam by swimming over limited distances by means of a skirt that it

abandoned on reaching dry land, to continue in the usual way as an ordinary tank. But in January 1944, production had still not attained levels required to complete the massive job in June. So when Montgomery showed them to Eisenhower on 27 January, Eisenhower immediately decided to have some made in the United States: inside 2 months 300 Shermans were fitted out as D.D. tanks and shipped off to England.

Besides these special tank formations that were to accompany the assault waves, beach

Special Churchill British tanks belonging to the 79th AD. equipped with slatted mats for driving over trenches and anti-fortress "shells".
(Canadian public archives.)

Tank equipped with a flail arm. A Sherman M4 antitank from the 79th British AD. equipped with a rotating drum fitted with chains designed to explode traps and mines 9ft in front of its caterpillar tracks.
(I.W.M. document)

Armoured British bulldozer.

sapper units were set up and trained in a wide variety of specialised tasks for recognising and destroying obstacles and mines (Bangalore torpedoes, etc.) as well as operating the beach equipment and arrangements for easing the advance of vehicles landing on dry, slimy or clayey sand to terra firma by unrolling metal matting, marking out beaches, etc.

After the Dardanelles, the Dieppe raid had taught that one could not hope to capture a port in serviceable condition. After any successful assault, a certain time would elapse for mine-sweeping, refitting of harbour facilities, repairs, reopening of communications, etc. to be carried out before it could receive even small craft.

However, the build-up of forces after the assault was an essential condition for success, and could not be achieved with sufficient speed merely over the beaches that had served in the initial assault. The idea therefore soon dawned notably on Churchill to create artificial ports with material prepared in advance on the English coast and brought across to France for assembly on site. In May 1942, Churchill ordered his Chief of Combined Operations, Admiral Mountbatten, to study how to go about building an artificial port, regardless of the difficulty. Such was the origin of the very secret project of the 2 Mulberry harbours. Each port consisted of fixed caissons

linked together with floating quays, and to the beaches with floating ramps. The elements were built in England, and could be towed by boat right up to the coast of Normandy to be sunk or anchored at a location north of Bayeux.

These elements would be brought into play just as soon as the beachhead had been widened enough to provide the harbour adequate security.

COSSAC had launched a project for an underwater pipe-line to supply troops ashore in fuel. Code-named "P.L.U.T.O" (Pipe Line Under The Ocean). The idea was pursued with a view to linking England under the Channel to the ports of Cherbourg, then Boulogne.

Even if full use were made of resources analysed above, so as to bring in as quickly as possible within the two first days a second assault wave already embarked on landing craft, followed by troops in landing ships that had again become available after taking part in the initial assault, the rate of arrival of Allied troops onto the beaches would remain lower than the possible rate of strengthening of German resistance with the transfer of reserves from inland. The extent to which German reserves might be thrown into the battle must therefore be carefully assessed and compared to Allied potential, because this was one of the vital problems specific to amphibious operations.

The Allied command was fortunately very well informed by spotter planes and the French resistance as to where the German divisions were stationed, and it established a table of comparative strength as follows:

DAY	GERMAN FORCES N° OF DIVISIONS	ALLIED FORCES N° OF DIVISIONS
D	6	8
D + 1	12	10
D + 3	15	13
D + 7	22	16
D + 10	27	18
D + 20	30	24
D + 35	37,5	30

At any given moment the German ground forces were liable to be numerically superior to the Allied forces. However the attacker requires not just equality in numbers, but numerical superiority.

Indeed troops on the defensive benefit from the protection and the camouflage of the lie of the land and their fortifications, familiarity with the terrain and the location of their gun emplacements, and last of all from the initial and subsequent steady supply of weaponry; whereas the attacker breaks cover armed and equipped with whatever his vehicles can carry. Any amphibious assault involves enormous extra difficulties due to the change of mobility type when under fire, unless surprise effect is achieved.

However surprise is too much to be expected when the attack is a long-awaited affair in all parts. This inferiority inherent to the very nature of the landing operation had to be remedied in every imaginable and possible way. In the first place, the superiority of both air and naval supporting fire had to offset numerical inferiority, by destroying or neutralising the enemy's defences. Secondly, the arrival of reserves, especially tanks, had to be hindered by destroying them, by blocking any movement, and maintaining uncertainty as to a possible second landing.

S.H.A.E.F. was therefore led not only to facilitate the assault, but actually to make it possible by:
– aerial preparation,
– organising support at the moment of the assault,
– implementing a deception plan,
– making use of Resistance activity in France.
These four points shall now be studied in more detail.

Pluto (" Pipe Line Under The Ocean "). Giant drum containing a flexible pipeline designed to bring the fuel required for the two campaigning armies over from England.
(I.W.M. document)

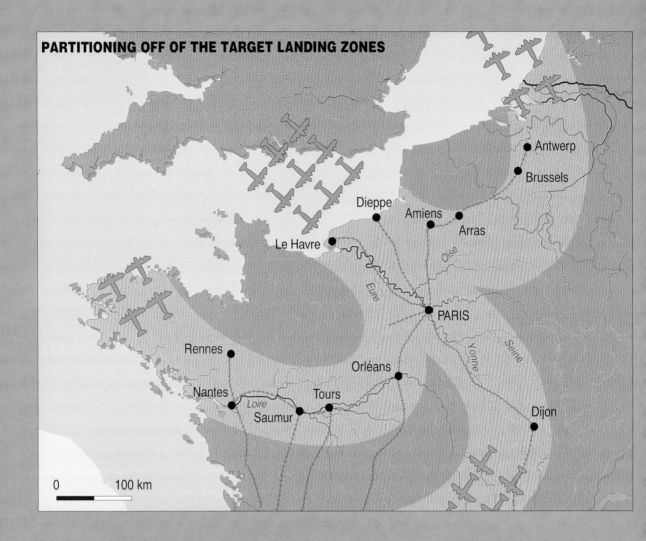

PARTITIONING OFF OF THE TARGET LANDING ZONES

Antwerp

Brussels

Dieppe

Amiens

Arras

Oise

Le Havre

Eure

PARIS

Yonne

Seine

Rennes

Orléans

Dijon

Nantes

Loire

Tours

Saumur

0   100 km

BOMBING RAID DESIGNED TO PARTITION OFF THE TARGET LANDING ZONES

The destruction of key bridges and rail hubs was an operation designed to sever the communication arteries used by German reinforcements and supplies.

The Normandy and Pas-de-Calais area was to be cut off in order to hamper the arrival of German reserves after the landing operation as far as possible.

This operation was performed by the two strategic air forces, British Bomber Command (Marshall Harris) and the 8th U.S. Air Force (General Doolittle) under the command of American General Spattz, Chief of the strategic American forces in Europe (Great Britain and the Mediterranean).

The tactical air forces brought in especially for the purposes of the "Overlord" operation were commanded by General Leigh–Mallory. General Tedder (British), Eisenhower's second in command, was in charge of co-ordinating all of the "Overlord" air operations.

The air bombing raids to cut off the landing areas started with the order to bomb Trappes station on the night of 6 and 7 March 1944.

CHAPTER NINE

LANDING AIDS:

SUPPORT - DECEPTION
THE CONTRIBUTION OF THE RESISTANCE

In the course of the year 1943, as we have seen, bombing raids to the Continent targeted on German industrial potential were gradually stepped up. The aircraft factories were one of the objectives of this operation, which contributed to gaining the supremacy that would be vital in June 1944.

Nevertheless, it was a distant target and brought no direct benefit to the Neptune assault. It was carried out under the authority of C.C.S. who sent over directives from Washington to *R.A.F. Bomber Command* (Air Chief Marshal Harris) and the U.S. *Strategic Air Forces* (General Spaatz). It was therefore outside the scope of General Eisenhower, whose only air resources were American and British tactical forces, both under Air Marshal Leigh-Mallory.

However, Eisenhower held the view that some methodical destruction of communications from Germany to the invasion beaches in Normandy had to be undertaken. Such action required the use not just of the tactical air forces but also strategic bombers, all acting as part of a single plan. Harris and Spaatz were reluctant to divert any part of their resources to this mission, in their view a secondary one, not in line with the appointed tasks they had received. Moreover Harris doubted the effectiveness of aiming at pinpoint targets such as railway junctions, road junctions and bridges, with bombers that until then had been attacking large industrial areas. For his part, Spaatz was using his Liberators and Flying Fortresses to carry out a methodical offensive against the

A R.A.F. Typhoon fight-bomber equipped with two 56lb bombs and eight 14lb SAP anti-tank missiles. The airplanes were formidable fighting weapons.
(I.W.M. document)

**D-Day: Bombing
of the Pointe de Hoc
by the 9th US Air Force A-20s.**
(U.S.I.S. document)

synthetic oil plants considering that, combined with the Soviet threat and the bombing of the Romanian oilfields from Italy, this was likely to put German industry in a spot. Thus neither was willing to use their air potential for the immediate benefit of *Overlord* until the final days before the assault.

This was not to Eisenhower's liking; he obtained from C.C.S. early in March that the Strategic Air Forces be placed under his "operational control" and he appointed his deputy, British Marshal Tedder to coordinate all operations of the air forces under Spaatz, Harris and Leigh-Mallory.

A complete plan was drawn up for the crippling of the railways. It covered the whole of northern France and Belgium, being designed to contribute to the "deception plan", the aim of which was to leave Hitler, von Rundstedt and Rommel uncertain as to the location of the future landing, Pas-de-Calais or Normandy.

As it turned out, such uncertainty was easy enough to maintain, both because of the structure of the French railway system, particularly dense in the North, and the construction, also in the North, of the V.-l launching sites that were obvious targets.

The railway destruction plan comprised 80 key targets, 39 of which were entrusted to Bomber Command.

The offensive began during the night of 6 to 7 March with a raid on the Trappes marshalling yard, methodically pursued, and followed by a sharp acceleration from 21 May, with attacks on bridges, viaducts and locomotives: the deception effect was kept up, as during the last week of May German reports noted 246 attacks north of the Seine as against a mere 33 to the south. The same reports mention in the same week 430 locomotives destroyed, and that out of the 2,000 in the northern region, 1,500 had been put out of action by air attacks: rail traffic was down to 13% of its January 1944 level.

Meanwhile the area between the Seine and the Loire was gradually cut off by the methodical destruction of the bridges over these 2 rivers - the prosperous Normandy sector was thus isolated from the rest of France: by 5 June, 18 of the 24 road and railway bridges across the Seine had been destroyed, 3 were under repair; and the remaining 3 were under constant threat, rendering them unusable for daytime convoys. The bridges of Paris however remained operational, and were in fact used by the Germans to move up their armoured reserves in June.

In addition to this long-distance activity against communications, this time for the immediate benefit of the assault, from D - 21 an intense offensive was launched against the airfields, coastal batteries, bridges, radar, etc., up to 130 miles inland from the northern as well as western coasts, again for purposes of deception.

The tactical air force responsible for these missions, and then for providing immediate support for the assault, numbered 2,434 fighters and bombers and 700 small and medium bombers. During the assault it was planned to maintain a constant density of:
- 10 fighter flights over the beaches,
- 6 flights in reserve ready to reinforce the ten others,

- 8 flights above the seaborne access channels between 65 and 80 miles off the coast of southern England.

During the 3 months prior to 6 June, 22,000 planes dropped 80,000 tons of bombs.

Being spread over such a wide area, as already indicated with reference to the railway destruction plan, the bombardment contributed in maintaining uncertainty as to the location of the projected landings; they were in fact part of the deception plan that COSSAC had devised and begun to implement since September 1943, the Fortitude plan.

The aim of Fortitude was to create in the German High Command the element of surprise necessary for the Allies to succeed, by concealing the truth, and by making it believe inaccurate information.

The truth was difficult to conceal, because the tremendous concentration of ground, air and naval forces in and around the British Isles could not escape observation by the Germans, even though they were hampered by the insularity of Britain, Allied air supremacy in the process of completion, and the freedom of the seas gradually re-conquered by the Allies in the Atlantic since June 1943.

The sheer size of the forces gathered was such that they had to be scattered across the entire country and in every port, which made it extremely difficult to identify the direction of the approaching attack. However, especially in the final weeks and days, the greater activity in port movements in the southwest of England would have to be camouflaged by artificial activity in the east. This was done. Likewise, radio activity was henceforth equally balanced in the southeast and the southwest so as to avoid the mere number of communications providing a clue to the Germans listening in, without their even needing to understand the

RAF Spitfires intercepted enemy hunter planes, patrolled behind enemy lines and dive–bombed tactical objectives on the army's orders.
(R.A.F. Museum.)

Aftermath of allied bombing raids on arsenal blockhouses.
(E.C.P.A. document)

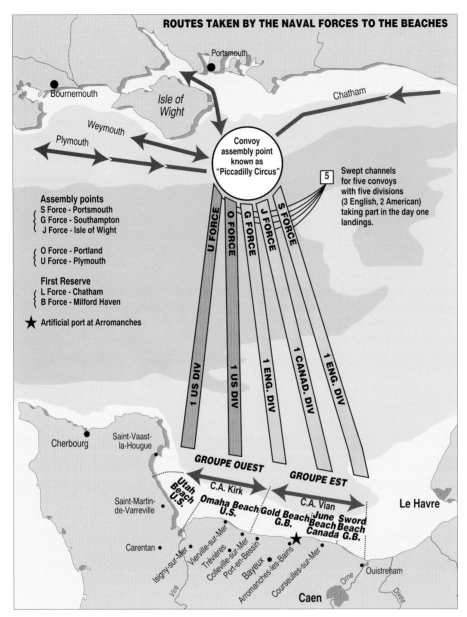

ROUTES TAKEN BY THE NAVAL FORCES TO THE BEACHES

ROUTES TAKEN BY THE
NAVAL FORCES TO THE
BEACHES:

• 5 forces set out following
destinations: Americans to
"U", "O" , British to "J", "G", "S".
• 2 rapid back–up forces: "L"
& "B".

Due to the distances involved
"U", "O" were already at sea
when Eisenhower dawn
postponed the landing
at dawn on 4 June
and were forced to return
to the ports where they had
been fitted out.
Each naval force was made up
of landing craft for the units,
small craft or amphibious
vehicles which were to be
launched once a line between
Cherbourg–Le Havre
and the back–up warships
had been reached.
The armada moving towards
the beaches off the Normandy
coast on the morning
of June 6 comprised
5 000 ships and 4 000 small
craft or amphibious vehicles.

messages. This camouflage would be continued until the landing and beyond, so as to
maintain the threat of a second landing in the
minds of the German commanders. Thus, during the night of the landing in Normandy, 105
R.A.F. planes and 34 smaller vessels of the
Royal Navy by unceasing movements and the
dropping of lures and balloons on either side
of Boulogne jammed German listening stations
and radar in the Pas-de-Calais.

These protective measures were reinforced
with attempts at intoxicating German

intelligence. False information was cleverly
passed on to journalists and neutral diplomats
living in England. The imagination of the
Allied intelligence services knew no bounds.
Thus in May 1944, a Montgomery look-alike
was conspicuously received very officially in
Gibraltar, so as to lend credence to the idea
that a landing was being prepared in Spain or
Provence, and which numerous Germans living in Spain did not fail to pass on to Berlin.

In June and July, the threat of a second landing in the Pas-de-Calais was maintained by

Admiral Ramsay.
(I.W.M. document)

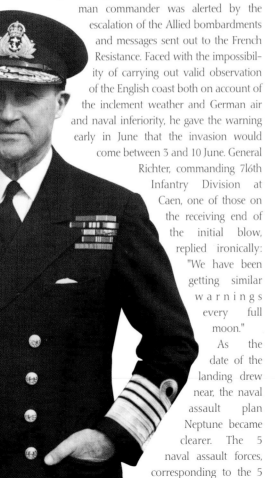

gathering together old landing-craft in the southeast of England and by dummy tank caterpillar tracks on the beaches of this part of the coast frequently observed by German spotter planes. Likewise General Patton, who did not take up his command until the end of July, made frequent marked visits to the Dover area so as to make believe that a second landing in northern France was being prepared under his command.

The postponement of *Overlord* from May to June also contributed to the deception. During the beautiful May weather favourable to a landing, von Rundstedt and Rommel repeatedly called their units onto the alert, till they reached stage when these routine alarms were ignored, and all the more so at the end of May when the weather became very bad, Rommel going as far as to state that there was little chance of a landing occurring before August. However, the German commander was alerted by the escalation of the Allied bombardments and messages sent out to the French Resistance. Faced with the impossibility of carrying out valid observation of the English coast both on account of the inclement weather and German air and naval inferiority, he gave the warning early in June that the invasion would come between 3 and 10 June. General Richter, commanding 716th Infantry Division at Caen, one of those on the receiving end of the initial blow, replied ironically: "We have been getting similar warnings every full moon."

As the date of the landing drew near, the naval assault plan Neptune became clearer. The 5 naval assault forces, corresponding to the 5 selected beaches on the Normandy coast, were assembled:

– American sector, Admiral Kirk:
  • force U for *Utah* at Plymouth,
  • force O for *Omaha* at Portland.
– British sector, Admiral Vian:
  • force G for *Gold* at Southampton,
  • force J for *Juno* on the Isle of Wight.
  • force S for *Sword* at Portsmouth.

2 support forces, B and L, were assembled close to Falmouth and Nore. To contribute to the deception, most of the merchant ships, many of which would later serve in bringing supplies to the Continent, were spread throughout the ports closest to the Thames and in Scotland.

12 flotillas of mine-sweepers were ready to open channels to the French coast at the last moment ahead of the landing-craft.

It was Admiral Ramsay who was responsible for bringing the ground forces ashore and for their immediate support. Rapid communications procedures and methods for requesting naval firepower for infantry support were developed. Designating targets was facilitated by detailed knowledge of the German defensive organisation obtained by reconnaissance work

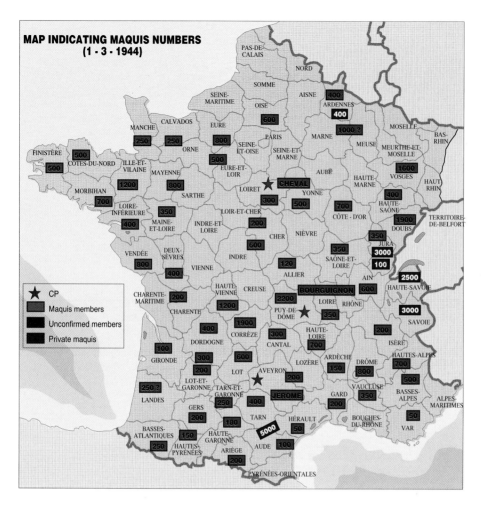

**MAP INDICATING MAQUIS NUMBERS
(1 - 3 - 1944)**

Legend:
★ CP
Maquis members
Unconfirmed members
Private maquis

THE FRENCH RESISTANCE AT THE TIME OF " OVERLORD "

The map shows estimates of French Resistance movement numbers. Difficulties in terms of liaison and uncertainty surrounding their assignments meant that command was unable to count on the actions of the Force Françaises from within the country although they were still able to provide solid assistance in the form of valuable intelligence to help it to devise its plans. As a result Resistance operations were and so, to a certain extent, were deemed to be supplementary to its plans. After the landing, however, intelligence continued to come in and its operations were easier to co-ordinate as a result of parachuting dropping the "Jedburgh" teams (90 men trained by 3 men in the British Special Forces) and American operation groups (11 in number made up of 4 men each from the Special Air Service) to the French resistance groups for the purposes of specific assignments. Support to the Resistance was stepped up as the landing operation drew closer. Operations reports estimate set figures for equipment parachuted into France (some fell into the hands of the German) during May 1944 at 80 000 machine guns, 30 000 revolvers, 17 000 guns and several thousand bazookas.

over a year or more under orders of COSSAC, and by French resistance networks.

It was planned that the various naval convoys set in motion at different times in function of the journey they had to cover should pass via a wide assembly point, "Area Z", nicknamed "Piccadilly Circus", in the English Channel, 20 miles southeast of the Isle of Wight, before heading off towards their respective beaches along 5 channels previously cleared by mine-sweepers.

Some figures illustrate the huge scale of the assault that would take place on 6 June and the logistical support.

The naval arrangement comprised 5,000 ships and 4,000 smaller vessels (for plying between the ships and the shore). Naval support was provided by 6 battleships, 2 monitors, 22 cruisers and 93 destroyers.

In the above description of the aerial bombardment, the assault plan etc., we have several times alluded to the part played by the Resistance in France, and also in Belgium.

Prior to *Overlord* the Resistance had 2 possible courses of action: to take part in operations to cut off communications channels, or to supply intelligence.

On the first point, General Koenig, present in London as Commander of the French Forces of the Interior, emphasised that the resistance could be used to sabotage the railways at less human cost to the local population than by aerial bombardment. Churchill explains in his Memoirs how difficult it had been to decide to

Propaganda poster.

Corrèze, summer 1944 (near Ussel): Bridge blown up by the Maquis after the landing in order to delay German troops coming up to Normandy from the South of France.
(E.C.P.A. document)

implementation made it too big a risk to entrust this task to the Resistance. Resistance activity could be considered only as a supplement restricted to particular special cases such as tunnels in the Jura, oil dumps in Rouen, sabotage inside power stations, etc.

On the other hand, among the unparalleled feats of intelligence gathering that we may quote - as many works have indeed quoted - pride of place has to go to the seizure, back in May 1942, of the plans of the "Atlantic Wall" under construction, from Cherbourg to Honfleur, by a resistant of the Brotherhood of Our Lady network (Confrérie Notre-Dame). Right up until the day of the landing, accurate information reached London regarding the fortifications, their occupation, also German troop activity and movements in France. And it was an unfortunate piece of bad luck, symptomatic nevertheless of the risks involved in Resistance work, that the stationing in the last days of May in the Bayeux-Isigny sector of the crack German 352nd Division went unnoticed; a division that the infantrymen of U.S. 1st Division (Major-General Huebner) had the

launch a systematic bombing campaign against the railways inevitably involving the loss of many French lives, and that it was only faced with the absolute necessity for the success of *Overlord* of hampering the German reserves moving up that such a decision was taken. The uncertainties of communications and

unpleasant surprise of finding themselves confronted with at Omaha. Apart from this one exception, the Allied command was perfectly acquainted with the German set-up and the possibilities of enemy intervention.

Immediately after the landing, the Resistance's plan of action was to be set in train by a coded radio message over the BBC. Intelligence continued to flow in. The coordination of Resistance activities and the link-up with the French Forces of the Interior were anticipated by the dropping of French and Allied parachute squads over Brittany during the night of the 5 to 6 June, and all over France in the days and weeks that followed (*Jedburgh* and *Operational Group* squads of the American *Special Air Service Troop* especially) to strike against communications channels converging on Normandy.

Of course, orders addressed to the Resistance were written in such a way that if they came to the knowledge of the German command, they would not give away Allied instructions, but, on the contrary, contribute if possible to the intoxication sought after as part of the deception plan.

Alongside all these intertwined preparation activities, deception, bombardment, intelligence gathering, reinforcements from the United States, the setting up of combined forces and Chiefs of Staff planning, personnel training and instruction were stepped up. Manoeuvres and firing practice continued at a steady rate. The men's degree of instruction was tested by carefully marked examinations, and by the state of their various equipment.

Training exercise led by Lieutenant Philippe Kieffer involving commandos who went on to land at Ouistreham on 6 June 1944.
(R.H.A. document)

24 June 1944: arrival of a French parachutist in Brittany.
(R.H.A. document)

Liaison between the combined forces, vital to bring effective rapid air and naval support for the ground forces down to the smallest echelons, was achieved by devising quick and easy procedures learnt through intensive instruction.

Combined exercises were carried out at sea near the coasts of England. They helped to weld a firm bond between the naval and ground troops that would carry out the amphibious assault. These exercises were occasionally disturbed by the German navy. At the end of April, during an exercise code-named Tiger in the Plymouth area, German E-boats, who thought incidentally that they were dealing with a convoy, sank 2 L.S.T.s, causing loss of human life. These exercises were very formative for the troops. They also revealed that during *Overlord* the German navy would still be capable of reacting although it had suffered a clear defeat in the battle of the Atlantic during the second half of 1943. Eisenhower, in his operations report, considered that in the first days, German resources comprised 5 destroyers, 10 torpedo boats, about fifty E-boats, about fifty "R" type torpedo-boats, 25 mine-sweepers and 60 miscellaneous vessels.

If as might be expected, the German command concentrated all its forces against the invasion, the number of submarines immediately available and within striking distance would increase to 130, and might reach 200 by D + 14.

These same reports mention the following assessments for the end of May "approximately 100,000 armed Frenchmen could enter into action at a signal given by London, not counting 35 to 40,000 armed "maquisards" only a quarter of whom had ammunition for more than a day's intense combat".

Kieffer Commando
(Forces Navales Françaises Libres/E.C.P.A.)

End of May 1944: mustering of US troops in isolated encampments along the south coast of England.

CHAPTER TEN

THE FINAL PHASE BEFORE THE ASSAULT:
WEATHER REPORTS - THE DECISION

In May the intense preparation directly centred on Overlord and begun on 1 January was finally completed. Its purpose, under the direction of Eisenhower, was to combine in a closely welded beam all the resources that resulted from convergent efforts made for close on 4 years by the Allies with a view to the invasion of Europe.

On 15 May, a briefing session took place, in the presence of Churchill, around Eisenhower with his deputies and his principal subordinates, for the Final Presentation of Plans for *Overlord*, and especially its amphibious side, Neptune.

Montgomery presented the plan for the ground assault. The initial articulation for the assault had been gradually worked out and fine-tuned in the course of the preceding months. It resulted from the imperative outlined above on the subject of the philosophy of the manoeuvre. More particularly the estimate of reinforcements

in troops and supplies coming directly from the United States via Cherbourg and the ports of Brittany necessarily involved General Bradley's American forces being placed in the west, and later on the exploitation of the breakthrough to be carried out by the as yet unformed U.S. Third Army commanded by General Patton.

Two beachheads were to be established on D-Day: one between the Vire and the Orne rivers, taking in Isigny, Bayeux and Caen; the other on the coast of the Cotentin peninsula, north of Vire. These two beachheads would not be joined up until D + 1 at the earliest.

Between D + 1 and D + 8, the beachhead would have to be widened westward, to the north-west and to the south, but hardly at all to the east and southeast. Caen and the open ground south of Caen would have to be solidly held (I British Corps), and be used as a stronghold with a

GERMAN FORCES IN NORMANDY ON 6 JUNE:

The line between the VII (General Dollman at Le Mans) and XV (General von Salmuth at Tourcoing) armies has moved eastwards of the Orne river between the 716th and 711th divisions.

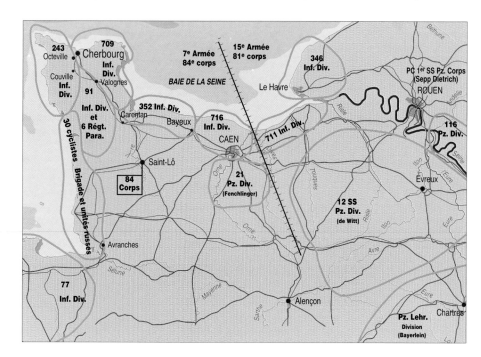

the Cotentin peninsula and make efforts to capture Cherbourg by D + 8 (General Bradley did not believe he could seize the port before D + 15).

Ground would then continue to be gained to the south with the help of Allied reinforcements, including the Canadian First Army and American Third Army (Patton), with the purpose by D + 50 of holding the Breton ports in the west, the Loire to the south, and a line Deauville-Tours to the east. The planned objective for D + 90 was the Seine, the Paris-Orleans gap, and the Loire.

Montgomery stressed the prompt and determined way that Rommel had certainly gone about reinforcing his defences in the 6 months since he took over command. Rommel's intention was to defeat *Overlord* on the beaches, deny any penetration, and to "prevent our tanks from landing by using his own tanks well forward". Thereafter he would "continue his counter-attacks" and

A parachutist from the British airborne troops pictured with a Horsa glider.
(I.W.M. document)

A mustering base for transportation forces serving the British airborne troops. Horsa gliders and their tow planes, RAF Halifax bombers are marked with black and white marker bands to denote "friendly" craft in the sky on D–Day.
(R.A.F. Museum document)

view to pushing back any counter-attacks by German tanks coming from Rouen, Paris or Chartres. By D + 9 V U.S. Corps and XXX British Corps would have to hold the high ground above Saint-Lô, Caumont and Villers-Bocage, to a sufficient distance in order to protect the artificial port (code-named Mulberry) set up at Arromanches from direct shellfire. VII U.S. Corps would secure

"combine them with a roping-off policy" and try to "hold firm on the important ground which dominates and controls the road axes in the bocage country."

These tactics of Rommel's had to be met with offensive eagerness to penetrate with armoured columns, and to get a good lodgement before the enemy could bring up sufficient reserves. This objective would be reached once the line Granville-Vire-Argentan-Falaise-Caen was firmly held. "We shall have to send the soldiers into this party 'seeing red'. They must see red. We must get them completely on their toes, having absolute faith in the plan; and imbued with infectious optimism."

This was the *crusader's spirit* referred to by Eisenhower in the title of the book that he was later to write, Crusade in Europe, and which was instilled in the troops sent forth to liberate the continent of Europe.

In the first days of May, ground units were directed to the port areas facing the naval forces, U, O, S, G, J, B and L, to which they were adapted. They were sealed off in their embarkation areas and their whereabouts was veiled in absolute secrecy. All communications were cut off with the outside world. They then received their missions and were supplied with very precise written and photographic information about their respective objectives. Many then noticed the resemblances with the training grounds on which they had been exercising. It was likewise for British 6th Airborne Division (Major-General Gale) and American 82nd and 101st Airborne (Major-Generals Ridgway and Taylor). The mission of British 6th Airborne to the east of the river Orne had been planned for a long time. The missions of 82nd and 101st Airborne were modified a week before D-Day in response to intelligence received from a French resistant signalling the movement of a fresh German division to Saint Sauveur-le-Vicomte where 82nd Airborne were due to be dropped. 101st Division received the mission to drop near the beach exits at Utah north of Carentan; 82nd in the Sainte-Mère-Eglise area. This modification had the advantage of reducing dispersion. This did not however reassure Leigh-Mallory, who again expressed his fears of failure to Eisenhower: German flak-guns, very close to Cherbourg, as well as inundations

Admiral Kirk,
Chief of the Western tactical
naval force.
(U.S.I.S. document)

and obstacles, might cause losses running as high as 80% of troops engaged. Nevertheless, Eisenhower maintained the operation, owing to the importance of the airborne operation for the beach exits from *Utah*, the link-up with *Omaha*, and the rapid conquest of Cherbourg.

Some units received special missions. The British 22nd Independent Parachute Company had to seize the Bénouville bridge across the River Orne 7 hours before the seaborne landing in order to secure the flank against the German reserves. The battalion of the Royal Ulster Rifles under Lieutenant-Colonel Otway would be dropped four hours before H-Hour, to the east of the mouth of the Orne, to seize the Merville battery to prevent its 150 mm guns pounding the beaches. In the parachute dropping-zones east and west, *pathfinder* reconnaissance teams were to be dropped a little after midnight to mark out the parachute and glider landing-zones. Finally 3 companies of American Rangers were detailed to seize the Pointe du Hoc, a high rock jutting up vertically above the Channel 2 1/2 miles west of *Omaha* beach on which stood a coastal battery covering *Utah* and *Omaha* beaches with its firepower.

These special missions had had several weeks' preparation with rehearsals on models of the objectives to be captured reproduced down to the finest detail.

Thus by the evening of 3 June, everything was ready for the airborne assault during the night of the 4 to 5 and the amphibious assault from 6.30 a.m. on the 5.

Then the drama of the weather began.

General Eisenhower had moved his headquarters to the Portsmouth area close to the ports from which the armada placed under his command would set forth for the mainland of Europe. It was there that on the evening of Friday 2 June, then the morning of Saturday 3, Eisenhower, his deputy Tedder, his Chief of Staff Bedell Smith, his main subordinates, Montgomery, Ramsay and Leigh-Mallory all met to hear the head of the team of meterorologists, Group-Captain Stagg of the R.A.F., who had forecast a deterioration in the weather after 1 June, with strong winds and rough seas. While naval force U was already on its way, at 3 in the morning, Stagg announced a worsening picture over the next few days with low thick cloud, fog and poor visibility, unfavourable for the parachute drops and naval and aerial support; also a swell making access to the beaches all the more difficult for the landing-craft, tanks and amphibious vehicles. Any postponement would be a grave matter since it would create a huge bottleneck of ships having to turn back and remaining loaded, those units due to follow in behind them having already taken their places in the ports of departure; the secret could no longer be kept. In any case, only 3 days in June were possible, 5, 6 and 7; a delay of several weeks until such time as the moon and the tide would again both be right together would jeopardise the sum-

Colonel Stagg who provided the forecasts necessary for General Eisenhower to set the date of the D-Day operation for 4 & 5 June.

Parachute supplies packs for the airborne units.

D–1: a British army chaplain conducts an ecumenical service for the troops.

mer campaign to the Rhine and the Ruhr; on the other hand, already full of risks in normal conditions, carrying out the amphibious assault with the weather so badly wrong could mean the failure of the entire invasion with dramatic consequences for the long-term future of Europe.

Calmly, and although Admiral Ramsay had observed that by nightfall force O would in turn have set sail, Eisenhower decided to postpone the decision till the meeting the following morning.

On Sunday 4 June, at 4 a.m., Stagg announced low cloud, gale force winds, and rough seas, with no expected change on Sunday, Monday or Tuesday. However a very slight and brief improvement might be possible on Wednesday 7. Eisenhower postponed the operation.

At 4 a.m. on Monday 5, whilst the storm raging over the camp, awash with rain, demonstrated that any assault launched that morning would have been disastrous, Stagg announced that an unexpected break in the weather over the Atlantic would bring a fair interval overnight until about the evening of Tuesday 6, with the wind dropping and improved visibility, after which the extremely violent storm would immediately return. This might prove sufficient to get a foothold on the shore, but the build-up would be extremely difficult.

Eisenhower made his decision at 4.15 a.m.: *Overlord* was on for the following day, 6 June.

Interrupted naval movements resumed their course immediately undetected by German aerial and naval observers, no doubt trusting in the bad weather and not very inquisitive.

The invasion was underway.

Eisenhower could only stand back and watch the unfolding of the scenario that had been prepared with all precision under his orders over the previous 4 months. On the afternoon of 5 June he paid a visit to the paratroops of 82nd and 101st Airborne Divisions that were to jump that night in what to his mind was a vital mission for the success of the operation.

Les sanglots longs
des violons
de l'automne
blessent mon cœur
d'une langueur
monotone.

The second part of this stanza by Verlaine was broadcast by B.B.C. at 8.15 p.m on 5 June. The first part broadcast during the night of 1-2 June had alerted certain members of the French Resistance. This second section informed the resistance fighters that the landing would take place within 48 hours and gave the signal for the French Forces of the Interior to launch their planned sabotage operations, particularly against communications networks.

General Eisenhower talking, at the end of the afternoon on 5 June, to parachutists of the 101st Airborne division anxious about their forthcoming night jump. Up to 75% of the parachutists could die. However, even with such a high price to pay, drops towards the rear of Utah beach were indispensable and would be key to the success of the "Overlord" operation.

(E.C.P.A. document)

CHAPTER ELEVEN

THE EVE OF D-DAY:

5 JUNE

When at 4.15 a.m. on 5 June, upon the announcement of a probable lull the next day in the storm currently raging, Eisenhower set D-Day for 6 June, movements for Operation Neptune were already underway. The naval convoys, which had been stopped and turned back on the morning of the 4 owing to the postponement of D-Day from the 5 to the 6, had taken to sea again, particularly the one bound for Utah, since it had the longest journey.

British Class X midget submarine.

Two midget submarines X-20 and X-23 had left Portsmouth on 3 June to identify Sword and Juno beaches 24 hours in advance, to remain underwater, surface at dawn on D-Day and, by pointing luminous signals out to sea, to guide convoys in to the two narrow beaches where it was difficult to get one's bearings. They were in place on the 4 for the landing set for the next day.

At 1 a.m. on 5 June, they were informed of the 24 hour postponement. They took up position on the sea bed opposite the coast, where they observed no movement to raise the alarm, and

Forces aeriennes françaises libres taking part in the D–Day aerial cover operations. Photo depicts the famous Lorraine group with an average–sized Boston bomber from R.A.F 342 Squadron.
(F.A.F.L. document)

kept their vigil until the moment came to carry out their mission at dawn on the 6.

On the afternoon of 5 June, Eisenhower called on the American paratroopers at their base making last-minute preparations before taking off for the Cotentin peninsula. Eisenhower later wrote that the decision to maintain 82nd and 101st Airborne's mission had been an even harder one than launching Overlord on the morning of the 6.

As soon as such an operation was envisaged, Leigh-Mallory, commander-in-chief of the air force, expressed doubts about the chances of success and reservations as to probable losses in aircraft and men. However on 25 May information was

American parachutists making preparations in England on the eve of D–Day.
(U.S.I.S. document)

received that a German division, the 91st, had been moved up to the west coast of the Cotentin, the projected dropping-zone of 82nd Division (General Ridgway). The decision was therefore taken to land this division 12 miles further east alongside 101st Division near Sainte-Mère-Eglise. But this meant that the 915 aircraft transporting the 2 divisions (including 96 with gliders in tow) would have to cross the entire Cotentin peninsula from west to east at less than 1,000 feet, over an area thick with flak-guns, before dropping their fighting troops in a heavily defended zone. Given the time needed to send in the waves of aircraft, the crossing would take 3 hours. Leigh-Mallory estimated that losses would be considerable, half of the planes and two-thirds of the gliders and troops transported. This operation was vital for the exploitation of the landing at Utah in the direction of Cherbourg, whose speedy capture was a key factor in the post-invasion build-up. On 28 May, in spite of renewed objections from his air force commander, Eisenhower decided to maintain the airborne operation whatever the risks, because he considered it an essential task. At least his decision on the morning of 5 June to set Neptune for the following day was taken on the advice and with the approval of the best and most well-informed experts.

In the gesture accomplished on the afternoon of 5 June appears Eisenhower's deep humanity: anxiety about what was to happen to the men he was sending into battle at great risk, and the certainty that their mission was vital for the success of the operation to restore freedom to the world that lay on his shoulders.

The huge Neptune-*Overlord* machine was on the move. The commanders who had set it in motion could now watch, powerless to intervene on the course of events until a certain period of time had elapsed. Everything rested initially on those who were to carry out the operation, down to the smallest units.

All day, in raging seas that caused seasickness among the combat troops being transported, the naval convoys headed for the appointed "Area Z", known familiarly as Piccadilly Circus. Air patrols provided constant surveillance against submarine and E-boat

Insignia of the combined operation designed by Lord Admiral Mountbatten in 1941.

Tract from the Supreme headquarters of the Expeditionary Allied Forces.

Les armées alliées débarquent

LE GENERAL EISENHOWER S'ADRESSE AUX PEUPLES DES PAYS OCCUPES:

PEUPLES DE L'EUROPE OCCIDENTALE !

Les troupes des Forces Expéditionnaires Alliées ont débarqué sur les côtes de France. Ce débarquement fait partie du plan concerté par les Nations Unies, conjointement avec nos grands alliés Russes, pour la libération de l'Europe.

C'est à vous tous que j'adresse ce message. Même si le premier assaut n'a pas eu lieu sur votre territoire, l'heure de votre libération approche.

Tous les patriotes, hommes ou femmes, jeunes ou vieux, ont un rôle à jouer dans notre marche vers la victoire finale. Aux membres des mouvements de Résistance dirigés de l'intérieur ou de l'extérieur, je dis : "Suivez les instructions que vous avez reçues ! " Aux patriotes qui ne sont point membres de groupes de Résistance organisés, je dis : " Continuez votre résistance auxiliaire, mais n'exposez pas vos vies inutilement : attendez l'heure ; où je vous donnerai le signal de vous dresser et de frapper l'ennemi. Le jour viendra où j'aurai besoin de votre force unie. Jusqu'à ce jour, je compte sur vous pour vous plier à la dure obligation d'une discipline impassible.

CITOYENS FRANÇAIS !

Je suis fier de commander une fois de plus les vaillants soldats de France. Luttant côte à côte avec leurs Alliés, ils s'apprêtent à prendre leur pleine part dans la libération de leur Patrie natale.

Parce que le premier débarquement a eu lieu sur votre territoire, je répète pour vous, avec une instance encore plus grande, mon message aux peuples des autres pays occupés de l'Europe Occidentale. Suivez les instructions de vos chefs. Un soulèvement prématuré de tous les Français risque de vous empêcher, quand l'heure décisive aura sonné de mieux servir encore votre pays. Ne vous énervez pas, et restez en alerte !

Comme Commandant Suprême des Forces Expéditionnaires Alliées, j'ai le devoir et la responsabilité de prendre toutes les mesures nécessaires à la conduite de la guerre. Je sais que je puis compter sur vous pour obéir aux ordres que je serai appelé à promulguer. L'administration civile de la France doit effectivement être assurée par des Français. Chacun doit demeurer à son poste, à moins qu'il ne reçoive des instructions contraires. Ceux qui ont fait cause commune avec l'ennemi, et qui ont ainsi trahi leur patrie, seront révoqués. Quand la France sera libérée de ses oppresseurs, vous choisirez vous-mêmes vos représentants, ainsi que le Gouvernement sous l'autorité duquel vous vous verez vivre.

Au cours de cette campagne qui a pour but l'écrasement définitif de l'ennemi, peut-être aurez-vous à subir encore des pertes et des destructions. Mais, si tragiques que soient ces épreuves, elles font partie du prix qu'exige la victoire. Je vous garantis que soient ces en mon pouvoir pour atténuer vos épreuves. Je sais que je puis compter sur votre fermeté qui n'est pas moins grande aujourd'hui que par le passé. Les héroïques exploits des Français qui ont continué la lutte contre les Nazis et contre leurs satellites de Vichy, en France et dans l'Empire français, ont été pour nous tous un modèle et une inspiration.

Ce débarquement ne fait que commencer la campagne d'Europe Occidentale. Nous sommes à la veille de grandes batailles. Je demande à tous les hommes qui aiment la liberté d'être des nôtres. Que rien n'ébranle votre foi — rien non plus n'arrêtera nos coups —ensemble, nous vaincrons.

DWIGHT D. EISENHOWER, Commandant Suprême des Forces Expéditionnaires Alliées

attacks; the German navy, reassured by the bad weather, did not show up. Whilst clearing access channels to the five beaches, mine-sweepers discovered newly-laid mines south of the Isle of Wight. The mines caused the first loss, that of the mine-sweeper Osprey, soon followed by the British destroyer Wrestler.

From his headquarters, Admiral Ramsay followed the progress of the convoys as they headed towards their beaches with a minimum of errors, and came in sight of the coast before dawn. At midnight, he reported that in spite of unfavourable weather conditions, which would however gradually improve later in the day (south-westerly wind force 5, heavy seas, poor visibility) and except for a minimal number of smaller vessels in difficulty, the 7,000-strong armada was sailing according to plan.

In the air, thousands of aircraft had been flying towards the Continent since 10 p.m.: bombers completing the job of cutting off Normandy, transporting and escorting the 3 airborne divisions, fighter bombers neutralising beach defence works.

At German Fifteenth Army headquarters at Tourcoing, the message broadcast by the B.B.C. to the French Resistance - the second part of Verlaine's stanza - had been overheard and understood: the invasion was imminent. The alarm was raised; however, due to some unexplained error, only Fifteenth Army was alerted, and not Seventh Army (General Dollman at Le Mans), garrisoned in the actual invasion zone.

As for Army Group B commander Field-Marshal Rommel, reassured by the weather forecast which was made a landing unlikely during the next few days, on the morning of 5 June, at the very moment when Eisenhower was taking the decision to attack the next day, he set off for Germany for a family celebration, intending to seek a private interview with Hitler in order to obtain the extra armoured reserves that he had been requesting for several weeks.

At Seventh Army headquarters, General Dollman, who throughout May had main-

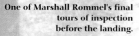

General Marcks commander the 84th Korps based at Saint-Lô during the D-Day fighting.

One of Marshall Rommel's final tours of inspection before the landing.

tained a constant state of alert and exhausted his troops in vain, had just temporarily relaxed his orders to give his men a much-needed rest.

He had summoned his principal subordinates to Rennes on the morning of 6 June for a war games exercise on how to react to a landing; these were General Marcks, commander of LXXXIV Corps (headquarters at Saint-Lô), and the commanders of the various divisions deployed along the Normandy coast, including General Falley, commander of 91st Division which had just been stationed at the western base of the Cotentin peninsula. On the way to Rennes, Falley, who had left that evening, was alerted by the endless drone of Allied planes; he turned back during the night: at the entrance to his headquarters he was killed with a burst of submachine-gun fire from American paratroops who had just landed.

It was a few minutes past midnight: *Overlord* was underway.

The 2nd U.S. ID completing its landing opening at Omaha. The beach has been successfully held. Photo depicts bulldozers, cranes, land artillery guns and towed anti-aircraft flak guns.

(R.H.A. document)

PART TWO

THE BATTLE
OF
NORMANDY

CHAPTER TWELVE

6 JUNE 1944, D-DAY:
THE ASSAULT

6 June R.A.F Stirlings parachute–dropping men from General Gale's 6th airborne division.
(I.W.M. document)

Major Howards responsible for capturing the lifting bridge over the canal at Bénouville since known as Pegasus Bridge.
(U.S.I.S. document)

Support from Major Howard's " Ox & Bucks " during the fight for "Pegasus Bridge" on the night of 5 to 6 June. Photo depicts the bridge over the Caen canal where it meets the sea at the top and the bridge over the River Orne at the bottom.
(Keel University.)

Left:
American troops on board a L.C.I. heading for Utah on 6 June 1944 protected by a barrage of balloons designed to foil the approach of enemy planes.
(R.H.A. document)

It is hard to say exactly where the airborne assault first began.

East of the mouth of the Orne, at twenty minutes past midnight, 6 gliders landed and the men that they carried promptly seized 2 bridges on the canal and the Orne at Bénouville.

Shortly afterwards, a few miles further north, 200 men landed led by Lieutenant-Colonel Otway, with the mission to seize the Merville battery with its guns trained on the beaches near the mouth of the Orne.

Finally, further east, pathfinders were dropped a few minutes later, to guide the landings of British 6th Airborne Division under Lieutenant-General Gale.

This division's mission was before dawn to hold the area west of the Orne in order to protect the flank of the landing zone, and prevent or delay any counter-attacks by the German reserves; the most powerful of these was to be expected from

elements of 2lst Panzer Division (General Feuchtinger) stationed to the south of Caen.

On account of the difficult weather conditions, the parachute drops were more widely dispersed than had been anticipated in the plans, especially spreading far eastwards. Nevertheless, after several hours, several days for some, sparse elements of 6th Division rallied and carried out their mission. The dispersion even presented the advantage of leading the German command into believing that the

D. Taylor, commander of the 101st US airborne division.
(U.S.I.S. document)

threat was greater than the actual threat posed by the 6,000-odd men of the division.

On the western flank, American 82nd Airborne (General Ridgway) and 101st Airborne (Colonel Taylor) carried out a similar mission also of great importance for the overall success of Operation Neptune. Landing simultaneously, one at Sainte-Mère-Eglise, the other a few miles further south-east, they were to muster at dawn, and join hands with VII American Corps and its leading division (U.S. 4th Division) due

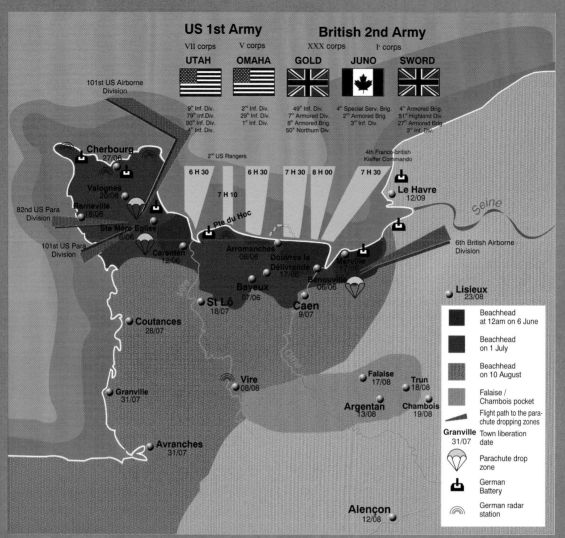

The Battle of Normandy. ("Le jour J et la bataille de Normandie", éditions Orep.)

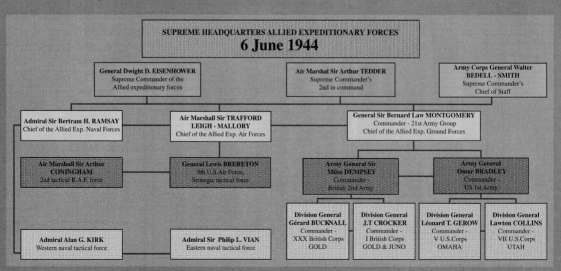

Parachute drops over Le Cotentin.
(R.H.A. document)

Insignia of the 101st US airborne division.

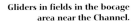

Gliders in fields in the bocage area near the Channel.

flew over the Cotentin, only 20 were lost. On the other hand the bad weather and flak-guns caused unexpectedly wide dispersion. 101st Division was spread over an area 25 miles by 15; by dawn Colonel Taylor had mustered 1,100 parachutists out of 6,600. 24 hours later he still had less than 3,000 men at his side.

82nd Airborne was more fortunate; three-quarters of the men dropped within a 3 mile square. At 12.30 a.m., Sainte-Mère-Eglise was taken and the Carentan-Cherbourg road blocked.

Unfortunately, the gliders failed to locate the landing-zones, and the heavy arms that they were carrying would be sorely missed in the hard battles that were fought in extended order against the units of German 91st Division.

As in the west, such dispersion had the advantage of drawing off the German forces, particularly 91st division, and diverting them away from their allocated task against the forces landing on the beaches.

101st Division, although hampered in rallying its troops, had dropped in a quieter area than had 82nd. Reinforced at first light from accurately piloted gliders, Colonel Taylor managed to seize a

to come ashore at Utah. Together the 3 divisions had to establish a beachhead strong enough to hold out, although isolated from the bulk of the forces disembarking on the beaches of the Calvados, on the far side of the marshy and flooded ground west of the mouth of the Vire and Carentan; they were also to set to work as quickly as possible cutting off the Cotentin peninsula along an east-west line and making headway towards capturing Cherbourg.

Although very dense, the anti-aircraft defences were less effective than Leigh-Mallory had feared; of the 805 transport planes that

battery position whose occupants had just been neutralised by an air attack, and to head off on horseback down the roads leading to the sea.

Some of his detachments mustered close to Sainte-Marie-du-Mont, and at 8 a.m. reached Poupeville, 5 miles from *Utah beach*. Further south the division came up against 6th German Parachute Regiment, and failed to reach the Carentan canal.

In Brittany at 1.10 a.m., 4 French reconnaissance squads each of 9 parachutists landed, 2 in Duault forest in the Côtes-du-Nord, under orders from Captains Botella and Deschamps, and 2 near Plumelec, on the Lanvaux moors in the Morbihan, commanded by Captains Marienne and Déplante. They had to prepare the way for 18 sabotage squads arriving the following night, and later the entire 2nd S.A.S. Parachute Regiment of Chasseurs of Free France, commanded by Colonel Bourgoin. Their mission was to cut off communications to German forces in Brittany liable to pour into Normandy, make contact with the Resistance, reinforce it, commit acts of sabotage to create a zone of insecurity on the flank of the invasion, and finally, to prepare a possible diversionary

German look-outs and soldiers in the beach blockhouses.
(E.C.P.A. document)

landing in southern Brittany so as to facilitate the capture of the ports.

At 1.10 a.m., German LXXXIV Corps (H.Q. at Saint-Lô) having been informed of the parachute drops over Caen and in the Cotentin peninsula, called a state of alert for all units deployed from the River Orne to Saint-Malo. The information was passed on to General Dollman's H.Q. in Le Mans and at 1.30 Dollman put Seventh Army on general alert.

At 2 a.m., von Rundstedt in turn was informed. From then on the German command was caught on the horns of a dilemma: was this landing in Normandy, of which the parachute drops were the first stage, the invasion, or was it merely a diversion, with the genuine invasion yet to follow in the Pas-de-Calais? This was a dilemma that could not be resolved for lack of precise information. German intelligence

The 1st battalion of the air infantry (S.A.S.) at Largo, Scotland (the arrow points to Corporal Bouétard killed at Plumelec during the night of 5 to 6 June 1944).
(E.C.P.A. document)

Horsa glider from the 6th Airborn

**German look-outs and soldiers
in the beach blockhouses.**
(E.C.P.A. document)

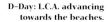

would cause and sustain the hesitations of the German command that began that very night. At 2.40 a.m., Seventh Army received a message from H.Q., West, at Saint-Germain, in which von Rundstedt stated that, according to his information, he did not consider this to be a major landing.

Nevertheless von Rundstedt put on alert for the benefit of Army Group B, - where Rommel's Chief of Staff, Speidel, was left in charge of operations in his absence -, 2 armoured reserve divisions, the large Panzer Lehr Division and 2nd S.S. Panzer *Hitler Youth* Division.

This was also the start of a lot of shilly-shallying and delayed execution resulting from the disastrous command structure enforced by Hitler. Von Rundstedt could not commit his armoured reserves without the sanction of the German Supreme Command (O.K.W.), i.e. Hitler himself. Von Rundstedt immediately requested permission to do this from Hitler who had just gone to bed, and whom nobody dared to wake, and only obtained his consent at 4 p.m. on the afternoon of 6 June, which was too late, as we shall see.

Also at 2 a.m., the German coastal defences were alerted. However no extra patrol was made along the sea, weather conditions being considered too unfavourable for a landing.

And yet the Allied armada was approaching. One force, bound for *Utah*, was ahead of schedule, and with a total strength of 1,000 craft carrying 30,000 men and 3,500 vehicles, at 2 a.m. was within 10 miles of its objective, the beach at Saint-Martin-de-Varreville.

reckoned existing forces in Great Britain at close on 100 divisions, whereas in reality there were only 50, and only 37 of these immediately available: thus by the time the beachhead had absorbed more or less all available forces in Great Britain, 45 days after 6 June, Hitler still thought that a second landing was possible. He was helped in this erroneous assessment by the Allied deception plan, Fortitude, which was carried on after 6 June: the concentration of dummy landing-craft, artificial radio activity, troop rotation movements in the S.E. of England, bombings carefully targeted on north-eastern France, orders to the French Resistance, etc.

The absence of any answer to this agonising dilemma of the "genuine" or "dummy" invasion

**D-Day: L.C.A. advancing
towards the beaches.**

THE NORMANDY LANDINGS

From midnight on, the night bombers flew over the naval assault forces. 1,135 planes of R.A.F. *Bomber Command* poured 5,853 ton bombs on ten clearly marked German coastal batteries. By first light, 1,083 bombers of U.S. 8th Air Force took over and dropped 1,763 tons of projectiles. A little before dawn, thanks to a break in the cloud layer at 4,000 feet that had allowed the parachute landings to proceed, light bombers and fighter bomber of Air Marshal Leigh-Mallory's tactical force went for individual targets and artillery positions along the coastline. They were in turn relayed by the guns of the naval support fleet, just before and during the landing, in close support of the infantry divisions as they came ashore.

However, low cloud hampered observation and shellfire; the German defences came in for less destruction than might have been expected in view of the tons of bombs and shells - except at *Utah* where the bombardment was effective. This accounts for the tough resistance encountered by the assault groups, in spite of the relative surprise for the German troops at seeing what was for them a fleet of unimaginable size and character suddenly emerge from the fog a few hundred yards in front of them.

The German command was also surprised by reports received throughout the morning from units engaged on the coast: coastal surveillance and radar installations had been blinded and had failed to warn of the thousands of Allied ships approaching unseen.

Between 1 and 4 a.m., while the armada was approaching the coast and with Allied bombers droning back and forth, only 9 radar installations and 18 out of 92 existing radio stations were in working order.

At von Rundstedt's H.Q. at Saint-Germain, incoming information only created confusion; it focused on the parachute landings broadly scattered from Troarn in the east to the western Cotentin and the centre of the area of activity of 9lst Division, whose commander had been killed at the start of operations near his H.Q., and close to where, it was later learnt, Major-General

Aerial photograph taken by a R.A.F. Mustang over Gold Beach at 9 o'clock on D-Day.
(Document - R.A.F. Museum, Hendon.)

Loaded L.S.T. (Landing Ship Tank) ready to land its cargo. Note the anti-aircraft protection balloons designed to foil attacks from enemy planes.
(R.H.A. document)

Gavin, commanding one of 82nd Airborne's *Regimental Combat Teams*, had just jumped.

Seventh Army's morning report, at 6.45 a.m., indicated large-scale airborne assaults during the night in the Orne and south Cotentin sectors, ending with the following sentence: "Air and naval reconnaissance since daybreak has yielded no fresh information."

15 minutes earlier the landings had started at *Utah* and *Omaha*.

D–Day at Utah Beach.

D–Day landing at Utah Beach.
(U.S.I.S. document)

Off these two beaches, from 2 a.m. the Allied shipping had come to a halt. The men climbed down from the ships into their flat-bottomed landing-craft; the special barges and amphibious vehicles went in: the first wave was due to hit the beach at *Utah* and *Omaha* at 6.30 a.m. Owing to reefs in the British zone, the assault would not reach the 3 eastern beaches until 7.30 a.m.

On the beaches, the German soldiers, alerted in their quarters, went to their combat positions facing out to sea; from 4 a.m. the bombers attacked them in successive waves, burying them in the dunes, cutting them off in their shelters or pinning them to the ground on the paths leading from their resting places to their combat stations.

When the dust from the explosions had settled, the German officers poked their heads out of concrete bunkers that had resisted the bombs or missed the shellfire which low cloud had prevented from adjusting properly. With no need for field-glasses, they gazed in amazement at the hundreds of ships of all sizes standing out on the narrow horizon of their embrasures, and even tanks and vehicles swimming in the water. They all went to man their guns and machine-guns pointed towards defences, stakes, mines, and barbed wire below the tide line. On the 5 beaches, the stage was set for the hard confrontation of men to commence.

It was at *Utah* and *Omaha* that the fighting began first.

At *Utah* the first wave hit the beach at exactly 6.30 a.m., not as planned on a level with Saint-Martin-de-Varreville, but 1 1/2 miles further south opposite a gap held by blockhouse W.5 (the one in front of the hamlet of La Madeleine, where the *Utah* museum now stands).

Resistance was on the whole fairly slight on this beach; together the foot-soldiers and their supporting D.D. tanks, most of which (28 out of 32) had swum safely ashore, went up and cleared the beach.

Having accidentally been put ashore too far to the south, these units had the good fortune to come in out of range of the German batteries at Montebourg and Saint-Marcouf, and faced a German combat unit of lesser quality than the one that they would have encountered had they landed on the prescribed beach. The

surprise effect produced by the amphibious tanks was out of all proportion with their actual firepower and gave added confidence to the determined advance of the American infantry.

General Roosevelt, who had come ashore in the first wave, decided to have the landing carried on where it had been started. Soon the sappers had cleared one beach exit, and then a second, 4th Division pouring through the breach. On attempting to broaden out northwards, they encountered stalwart resistance, but pursuing westwards made rapid progress. By 1 p.m. they had joined up with parachutists of 10lst Airborne Division at Sainte-Marie-du-Mont, at Poupeville, near Saint-Martin-de-Varreville. For the rest of the day, disjointed fighting broke out over a vast battlefield between the grenadiers of German 91st Division and American paratroops of 101st Airborne who rallied and consolidated their link-up with infantrymen of 4th Division who had now come ashore, and also the still scattered and isolated elements of 82nd Airborne. Behind this screen, the landing of 4th Division proceeded.

To the south, the valiant 6th German Parachute Regiment under Colonel von der Heydte barred the route to Carentan and counter-attacked: one of their battalions managed to reach the centre of the zone occupied by American paratroops at Turqueville, not far from Sainte-Mère-Eglise, held by 82nd Airborne since soon after midnight.

Before noon, a perhaps more optimistic message than was warranted by the actual situation informed General Bradley on board Admiral Kirk's flagship, the cruiser *Augusta*, that the landing at Utah was proceeding satisfactorily: "beaches cleared of obstacles. Roads under construction. Little opposition..."

Information received from *Omaha* was less encouraging. The beach was inherently less favourable: it was immediately bordered by sand dunes and escarpments, and on a third of its length by a small, smooth-edged sea-wall. In the dunes concrete gun emplacements had been fitted; at either end, near Vierville and Colleville-Sainte-Honorine, sheer bluffs closed in and flanked the beach. The rough seas were particularly violent along this long open

Generals Arnold (Air) and Bradley (US 1st Army) with Eisenhower, Supreme Commander of the Allied Expeditionary Forces on board the American D–Day command ship the U.S.S. "Augusta".
(R.H.A. document)

116th R.I. from the 29th U.S. I.D at H–Hour in Easy Green sector on Omaha Beach.
(R.H.A. document)

On the beaches of Vierville and Saint-Laurent, a fierce battle was immediately engaged. Landing-craft and troops were caught while still in the sea in the automatic gunfire of German 716th and 352nd Divisions. Unlike the former, the latter was a division of high quality and had been moved up to the coast at the end of May unbeknownst to the Allies, who had failed to receive a warning message from the French Resistance; this brought the number of battalions in position between Bayeux and Isigny to 8 instead of the 4 the Allies had been expecting.

The sappers worked miracles destroying obstacles, placing Bangalore torpedoes, cutting wire, blowing up mines that the low tide had fortunately made clearly visible: the tide was rising, leaving the American infantry, in growing numbers due to the arrival of the follow-up wave, an increasingly narrow space pounded by German shells.

6 June 1944. The difficult breach of the low wall defences at Omaha Beach and climb up to the dunes above.
(E.C.P.A. document)

D-Day: men trapped on Omaha Beach (1st US Division)
(U.S.I.S. document)

D-Day: the first wave of attack of the 1st US division trapped on Omaha Beach.
(U.S.I.S. document)

northern sea front and rendered navigation particularly hazardous for the smaller vessels and amphibious vehicles.

Major-General Huebner (1st Division) was to land 2 *Regimental Combat Team*, 1st and 29th Divisions, later reinforced by the remnants of both divisions, to widen the beachhead westward towards Isigny (1st Division) whilst 29th (General Gerhardt) would attempt a junction with the British in the Port-en-Bessin area. It was hoped that by nightfall on D + 1 a beachhead some 15 miles long and 6 miles deep would have been established.

Launching landing-craft and amphibious vehicles at 3 a.m. 11 miles offshore in heavy seas was extremely difficult. One of the two D.D. tank battalions decided not to put to the water and to take the tank carriers right up onto the beaches. The other launched its tanks, perhaps too far out in the rough sea, and only 2 out of 29 made it safely to the beach. The destruction of the German defensive organisation by air and naval fire-power had been very incomplete owing to poor visibility.

The American units suffered heavy losses, caught between the water and the concrete wall, where close contact with German pockets of resistance made naval artillery support difficult. The situation remained critical until noon: General Bradley on board the *Augusta* felt with anxiety that the moment was fast approaching when he would have to consider re-embarking.

In the German pillboxes, soldiers, 17-year-old youths and veterans of the Russian campaign, aimed and fired calmly, in the knowledge that they would run out of ammunition with no hope of fresh supplies getting through in the face of Allied air superiority.

As from 9.30 Major-General Huebner called upon the navy to bring their firepower to bear on German strong points, even at the risk of hitting certain sections of his own troops.

At 12.30 p.m., under the impetus of some American officers, notably General Cotta and Colonel Canham, and courageous sappers who worked desperately at the beach obstacles and mines, combat groups opened breaches in the "wall", in the sand dunes, in the German defences. Vierville, to the west, was taken, then in the evening access routes were opened to Colleville and Saint-Laurent.

Out of ammunition, the decimated, exhausted German soldiers left their pillboxes in the gathering dusk, and withdrew behind the dunes, hoping to find the tanks of the panzer divisions that their stalwart defence on the beaches should have given time to arrive; the next day they would throw the enemy back into the sea, for, although he had indeed managed to get a foothold, on the evening of

this first day he was confined within a narrow and precarious beachhead.

The day's fighting cost 800 men of 116th Regiment of 29th Division in the west, and a third of the brave men of the heroic Colonel Taylor's 16th Regiment, which managed to seize Colleville just before nightfall.

Midway between *Omaha* and *Utah*, the sheer cliff at the Pointe du Hoc dominates the sea..

The cliff was topped by a battery in a concrete casemate. It had to be taken in order to remove the threat that it brought to bear upon the beaches.

Such was the mission entrusted to a special American unit, the 2nd Ranger Battalion. In the

D–Day: Colonel Rudder's rangers at the foot of the cliff at Le Hoc. Ladders and grappling hooks were used to scale them under enemy fire.
(U.S.I.S. document)

days leading up to the attack, the Pointe du Hoc was subjected to massive bombardments and its guns had been taken out and aimed towards the west.

The position at the cliff top remained an important one however, and a difficult one to capture.

From 7 a.m. the Rangers scaled the cliff using firemen's ladders installed on barges, and guns to fire grappling irons and ropes, with the naval artillery in close support. The Rangers managed

La Pointe du Hoc – theatre for American ranger combats on 6, 7 and 8 June.
(U.S. Army document.)

Advanced first aid post on Omaha Beach.
(U.S.I.S. document)

**G.I.s at the foot of the cliff
at the Pointe du Hoc.**
(US Army document.)

**D + 1: rangers
from the 2nd battalion
rounding up prisoners.**
(U.S.I.S. document)

**6 June.
The landing gains pace
at Sword Beach.**
(R.H.A. document)

to capture the headland: all day long and again on the following day, they would fend off German counter-attacks. For two days, a Homeric battle was fought on this piece of rock.

On the Canadian and British beaches, from west to east, *Gold* between Le Hamel and La Rivière, Juno from Courseulles to Bernières and Saint-Aubin-sur-Mer, and *Sword* from Lion to Ouistreham, the landing did not begin until 7.30 a.m. owing to the presence of outcrops of rock offshore.

The assault was to be carried out by the British Second Army under Lieutenant-General Dempsey with 3 divisions, 50th on *Gold*, 3rd Canadian on *Juno*, 3rd British on Sword, each division with 2 leading brigades and 2 follow-up brigades in close attendance.

The ambitious objective to be achieved by D-Day evening was the Bayeux-Caen road, including both towns, and between the two the Carpiquet airfield west of Caen.

Gold beach, on either side of Asnelles, in the centre of the invasion zone halfway between the Cotentin and the Orne river at Caen, was flanked by sheer cliffs. The task of 50th Division therefore appeared hazardous, in spite of the preliminary

softening up this beach had received like all the others: aerial bombardment in the second part of the night, naval shellfire from first light right until the last minute before the assault. With close support from flail tanks and D.D. tanks that came in alongside and in places ahead of the infantry, the British brigades set foot on shore at 7.30 a.m. at la Rivière and Le Hamel, knocking out the German pillboxes and beach obstacles one by one.

It was a hard battle for the men coming back onto dry land. They had disembarked in the water, suffering from seasickness on account of the swell being particularly strong along this stretch of coast. The reefs cut the rising tide.

However by 11 a.m. 7 routes inland had been opened. The tanks poured through, and took the village of Creully. Armoured patrols burst in everywhere behind the German defences that still resisted, notably at Le Hamel, firmly held by the solid and unexpected 352nd Division; they moved forward in the east to Bernières to make the junction with Canadian 3rd Division; they pushed boldly southwards, reached the outskirts of Bayeux, followed the road from Bayeux to Caen at Saint-Léger and blocked the road from Bayeux to Arromanches; this last village would be soon occupied. The *Mulberries* were already on their way from various English ports for an artificial harbour to be set up there as quickly as possible. On the evening of 6 June, a naval

commando corps even managed to reach the top of the high ground south of Port-en-Bessin nearly 12 miles from its landing place and only a few miles from the Americans at Omaha. By evening the beachhead of 50th Division was 6 miles long and 6 miles deep, touching Bayeux and holding under its shellfire the Bayeux-Caen road, of vital importance for German reserve movements.

On *Juno beach*, the task of the Canadian 3rd Division was complicated by the presence of offshore rocks and a very heavy sea.

Also some of the landing-craft were late ashore. D.D. tanks were not launched until they were within 660 yards of the shore whence they swam

Top left :
A L.C.T. which has finished landing its armoured vehicles on Gold Beach, H + 45.

Top right:
Gold" Beach.
7.30 am on 6 June. The 50th British Northumberland division landed on the long beach of Asnelles at Ver–sur–Mer to the east of Arromanches. A German blockhouse was situated on the cliff where the orientation table now stands (position from which the photo has been taken) which overlooked and fired out over the beach.

6 June 1944.
46th Royal Marine Commando landing at Sword Beach.
(E.C.P.A. Document)

D-Day at Juno Beach: the Royal Canadian Navy at Bernières-sur-Mer.
(Canadian public archives.)

H + 2 – Bernières: the La Chaudière regiment rediscovers its roots.
(Canadian public archives.)

H + 3 on 6 June. Canadian 9th brigade land on "Juno" near Bernières.
(Canadian public archives.)

onto the beach: the sea being so rough, others were disembarked directly onto the beaches. Some hard fighting took place between Courseulles and Bernières and opened gaps through which surged the tanks which had landed, in close formation with the infantry and giving them good support with their well-aimed firepower. Due to the initial delay and the arrival of the follow-up waves exactly on schedule, the beaches were becoming rather congested. At 9.30 a.m., Bernières was cleared of all German resistance, and the southward advance had begun. In spite of initial difficulties due to the appalling weather, at day's end this Canadian division had come the closer to achieving its planned objective. The

beachhead was by now 6 to 8 miles deep: the junction in the west had been made with 50th Division and the 2 beachheads were firmly bonded: Caen was in sight; 2 battalions were within 3 miles of the city; the tanks had even touched the Caen-Bayeux road in places, but being isolated without infantry, had not stayed there.

In the extreme east, on *Sword*, British 3rd Division had a demanding task. Its objective was Caen, while the Canadian division on its left would be heading for Carpiquet.

Major-General Rennie commanding the 3rd Division was less anxious about the resistance to the landing that he would have to face from the ineffective German 716th Infantry Division than the possibility of a counter-attack being launched by 21st Panzer stationed to the south of Caen before he was firmly enough entrenched on Norman soil to resist. It was precisely to meet this danger that Major-General Gale's 6th Airborne had landed during the night in a flanking position

east of the Orne, deployed as far as Troarn and the River Dives and, as we have seen, had seized the vital bridge at Bénouville shortly after midnight. By the time 3rd Division was coming ashore, Gale had set up his H.Q. at Ranville, two miles east of this bridge, and his elements were scattered over a wide area, due to difficulties encountered with the parachute drop.

After 21st Panzer Division, 12th S.S. Panzer, garrisoned west of Evreux, could also intervene rapidly and considerably hinder the consolidation of the beachhead that would have to include Caen as quickly as possible.

Rear-Admiral Vian, commanding the naval force responsible for landing 3rd Division now turned his attention to the coastal batteries and

coastal defence launches based at Le Havre, as well as on any U-boat activity. However neither the coastal batteries nor the U-boats showed up.

Only a single patrol of 4 E-boats ventured to tackle the huge Allied fleets and managed to torpedo and sink the Norwegian destroyer *Svenner*; this would be the only loss caused by enemy naval offensive action.

In spite of the difficulties arising from the heavy seas, tanks and infantrymen disembarked against resistance neutralised by particularly dense and effective bombardment. 21 of the 25 D.D. tanks put to water arrived on the beach without mishap, except navigational, and provided the infantry with good support. Three beach exits were quickly opened; at 9.30, two miles from the beach, Hermanville was captured, not far from Périers Rise, held by infantry of 21st Panzer Division. At the same time fighting was engaged to clear the Ouistreham area - where among others Commandant Kieffer's French commando came ashore - , seize Colleville and attempt the

Pegasus Bridge – the bridge at Bénouville. It was captured at 0h25 by Major Howard and his men dropped by glider less than 50 metres from the bridge (to the right of the photograph).

Admiral Vian, R.N.

Pegasus Bridge.

Glider landings to the north-east of Caen (combat zone of the 6th British airborne division). (R.H.A. document)

Philippe Kieffer.

link-up on the Orne with paratroops of 6th Division: this was achieved at 1.30 p.m.

It was not till early afternoon, owing to the delay in the landing of tanks on a congested beach laboriously cleared by the engineers, that fighting began for the capture of Périers Rise from the summit of which Caen could be seen.

Further west, a British brigade had also been held up in landing and had failed to make much progress along the coast towards the Canadian beach.

Further east, advancing along the Orne and from 1 p.m. via Colleville, one British regiment reached Bréville at 4 p.m., less than 3 miles from Caen on the Ouistreham-Caen road; at the spearhead, they saw 24 German tanks appear ahead of them. With the road to Caen apparently open, the decisive battle with 21st Panzer Division was engaged.

As has already been stated, 6 panzer divisions were garrisoned in Rommel's Army Group B sector. From the point of view of administration, training and logistical support, these 6 divisions were under orders from General Geyr von Schweppenburg of Panzer Group West, who took his orders directly from von Rundstedt. For tactical purposes, 3 of these divisions (21st Panzer near Caen, 116th Panzer on the Seine west of Paris, 2nd Panzer near Abbeville) were responsible to Rommel, through the new panzer corps in the process of being set up, XLVII Panzer Corps. The three other divisions - Panzer Lehr near Le Mans, 12th S.S. Panzer near Evreux, and 1st S.S. Panzer near Antwerp - were under the command of II S.S. Panzer Corps (S.S. *Obergruppenführer* Sepp Dietrich), whose H.Q. was at Rouen. These made up von Rundstedt's strategic reserve which could not be committed without Hitler's authorisation. Added to this complicated chain of command involving 7 commanders, von Rundstedt, Geyr von Schweppenburg, Rommel, 2 panzer corps commanders and the 2 commanders of Fifteenth and Seventh Armies responsible on the ground for the coastal defences, was the fact that on the morning of 6 June, 3 commanders were absent from their headquarters: Rommel was at home at Heerlingen near Ulm; Dollman, commander of Seventh Army, was away from his H.Q. at Le Mans to oversee an exercise at Rennes; and Sepp Dietrich was in Brussels.

At 1 a.m., Feuchtinger, commanding 21st Panzer, was informed of parachute landings in the region of Troarn, 10 miles east of Caen. He gave orders to his 2 infantry battalions stationed on either side of the Orne to engage in battle against the parachutists; he sent out reconnaissance missions to the south of Caen against any paratroops that might have landed there as well. In the absence of his commander, Rommel's Chief of Staff, Speidel, was reluctant to move the panzers, and so they remained in the Falaise area. Not until 6.45 a.m., after speaking to Rommel on the telephone, did Speidel put 21st Panzer at the disposal of Seventh Army for the benefit of LXXXIV Corps under General Marcks (H.Q. at Saint-Lô), whose orders would not reach Feuchtinger until 8 a.m.

Meanwhile a part of Feuchtinger's panzer force began to make a move east of the Orne against paratroopers of British 6th Division. No other panzer division was available, since von Rundstedt was still waiting - as he would do so until 4 p.m. - for Hitler, who had not yet been informed of the landing, to authorise him to use the armoured reserves, of which the 2 closest were 2nd S.S. Panzer and Panzer Lehr.

Yet the landings, about which von Rundstedt's information was very sparse, had already begun and were developing between the Orne and the Cotentin.

At 10.30 Feuchtinger, the only commander available, was ordered to cross his entire division over to the west bank of the Orne, and intervene between Caen and Bayeux. His forces were scattered; some of his infantry and assault guns were committed against the paratroops east of the Orne; his 2 battalions stationed N.W. of Caen had been fighting since morning in the area around the bridge at Bénouville; the remaining one, the antitank battalion, equipped with highly effective 88 mm guns, had been placed under the command of 716th Division, and one section was holding firmly onto Périers Rise whilst the other had been called out to help further west, where it was busy containing the Canadian threat to the Caen-Bayeux highway.

Tank movements were rendered hazardous as Allied planes attacked with renewed effectiveness in the daylight and during breaks in the cloud. Crossing Caen took time and it was not until 3 p.m. that the panzer regiment reached the northern outskirts of Caen, there to receive from the lips of General Marcks himself the order to counter-attack as far as the sea.

The counter-attack finally came from 21st Panzer, a fine division in the glorious tradition of the *Afrikakorps*, but already divided and diminished before the battle had even commenced; in fact the only regiments to take part were the Divisional Panzer Regiment, 22nd Panzer Regiment and a mobile battalion of 1st Panzer Grenadier Regiment. The panzer charge towards Périers was led by Colonel von Oppeln-Bronikowski, a sophisticated and highly skilled horseman and a gold medal winner at the 1936 Olympic Games, as well as a valiant tank fighter in Poland, France and Russia where he was wounded and became the 536th member of the German army to add oak-leaves to his Iron Cross.

In the morning the British had been able to set up their anti-tank guns on the slopes of Périers Rise and to the west, between Colleville and Biéville, only just been captured and now in flames. The clash with 50 German tanks was

The Panzer Colonel von Oppeln Bronikowski responsible for commanding the counter-attack by his 22nd armoured regiment which approached the coast on the evening of 6 June.
(Bundes Archives, Koblenz.)

Germans bringing in a Tiger tank by rail. Belgium, end of June 1944
(E.C.P.A. document)

extremely violent, 22nd Panzer Regiment losing 16 tanks on Périers Rise. Von Oppeln-Bronikowski had to give up any hope of reaching the coast; but neither could he retreat, because on his left the grenadier regiment had broken through and reached the coast at Luc-sur-Mer and Lion-sur-Mer between the British and Canadian beachheads.

The regiment dug in on the spot when at 9 p.m. before dusk fell, the Allied air force bombers came to pound the German advance on Douvres, Luc and Lion.

For the Allies had enjoyed total supremacy in the air all day. This had been demonstrated over and over, at every break in the cloud, in supporting the disembarking forces, and in attacking communications and German reserve movements. It again intervened very savagely at the end of the day to the east of Caen against a tank group commanded by S.S. Kurt Meyer of 12th S.S. Panzer. Von Rundstedt, still awaiting Hitler's permission to use the panzers, had sent them on towards Lisieux in the morning, then in the afternoon towards Evrecy 10 miles south-west of Caen, with the mission to join 21st Panzer and together repulse the enemy forces that had penetrated west of the Orne. From Lisieux to Evrecy, the armoured column had been subjected to constant aerial attack, had had to stop many times and leave the road, to the point that it advanced at an average 4 miles per hour; they reached Evrecy at midnight, their fuel tanks drained by the repeated diversions, slow running and frequent stops; at a fuel dump near Evrecy they found the fuel drums in flames, destroyed by Allied planes.

D-Day ended with a demonstration of Allied air superiority.

At the same time as the leading elements of the 21st Panzer counter-attack were being taken to task, at 9 p.m., 248 gliders managed, with the appropriate escort, to carry on through the German *Flak* to bring 6th British Airborne the reinforcements in heavy equipment and ammunition that would allow Major-General Gale to establish a firm foothold east of the Orne.

According to General Eisenhower's operations report, throughout the day of 6 June, the strategic air forces dropped 10,395 tons of bombs in 5,809 sorties, while the tactical air forces undertook 5,276 sorties in direct support of the forces engaged.

The situation on the evening of D-Day was not as had been planned, which notably included the capture of Caen and Bayeux. Nevertheless the 5 beaches were firmly held. The expected counter-attack by 21st Panzer had indeed taken place; what would have been the most important event of the day, had it been launched earlier, could have jeopardised the success of the landing: as General Marcks told Colonel von Oppeln-Bronikowski at around 3 p.m., on giving him his mission: "The future of Germany may very well rest on your shoulders. If you don't push the British back we've lost the war."

His partial failure decided the outcome of the invasion. Caen, however, was not captured and

Continuation of the landing operations after the neutralisation of German defences at Utah Beach.
(R.H.A. document)

the battle for Caen would last another 2 months.

In the centre, the beachheads were not all joined up: there was a gap inside the British sector between the beaches of the Canadian and British 3rd divisions, where German forces again reached the coast with their backs leaning firmly against the battery at Douvres which dominated the entire plain of lower Normandy and which held out until 17 June. On the other hand, the junction between the British and Canadian beaches at *Gold* and *Juno* was achieved, and reached as far inland as Bayeux. The American *Omaha*, bridgehead, which had proved so difficult to establish throughout the morning, had been widened in the afternoon in the western sector. No junction was made between *Omaha* and the British *Gold beach*. However a British naval commando had attained the boundary of the 2 British and American sectors at Port-en-Bessin. The Arromanches zone, the site of the future artificial harbour to be built from gooseberries and scuttled blockships that were already on their way to their destination, was already out of the range of infantry fire, if not yet artillery fire.

The boundaries of the beachhead established from *Utah* of were ill-defined.

Beyond the perimeter held by the forces of U.S. VII Corps, dispersed paratroop elements fought bravely in isolated battles that considerably extended the area of insecurity and uncertainty for the Germans.

The German command had received little reliable information all day, on account of the communications chaos resulting from intense Allied bombings. It only heard of the landing in the Calvados after 9 o'clock, and even then the little information it received was inaccurate. In his operations report, Eisenhower wrote in a statement based on German archives captured later: "It was not until 1600 hours that [Seventh] Army learned of the *Utah* seaborne assault."

After receiving reassuring reports as to the progress of defensive against the airborne troops, LXXXIV Corps had also made a premature announcement to the effect that the landing at Saint-Laurent had failed.

The main danger appeared to the German command to come from the landings close to the Orne with the Cotentin operation no more than a diversion.

Thus ended the first day of the Allies' return to the continent of Europe, 4 years after the Dunkirk evacuation.

The ambitious objectives of Bayeux and Caen, with its open ground and its airfields, were not attained. Ahead of the central beachheads, lay the bocage, a totally unknown quantity. The situation appeared precarious. Nevertheless a lodgement area had already been established of such a size and with enough troops that it could no longer be wiped out. The Allies had gained a foothold on the Continent.

132,715 seaborne troops had come ashore plus an additional 15,000 Americans and 7 000 British who had landed in the midst of the enemy defences from 2,395 planes and 867 gliders.

Thus, in spite of the Atlantic wall, over 156,000 men had set foot on French soil on the first day of the campaign.

Casualties suffered were in the order of 2,000 killed and 9,000 wounded, not counting 1 thousand missing, a certain number of whom would turn up in the days following.

The cadence at which the battles were fought on this first day was proof of the quality of the German soldier. Taken by surprise, cut off with no communication possible with their commanders, subjected to intensive bombardment, with no support from their ineffective air force, the German infantry everywhere put up stout resistance. They used the terrain well, fired well, recovered quickly, and resisted every foot of the way. Clearly some from hard battles awaited the Allies in the days to come if they were to widen their beachhead.

The German command had put its finger on its two essential weaknesses: the loss of its

Omaha, D + 1.
The low tide uncovers the defences put in place by the Germans such as spikes, tetrahedrons, some of which are mined. Allied vehicles and the bodies of dead soldiers are still lying on the beach.
(R.H.A. document)

" Chaos ", the German look-out post built on two levels on the edge of the cliff at Longues-sur-Mer, between Arromanches and Port-en-Bessin. It was designed to fire its four-piece 152 anti-ship artillery over the Baies de Seine between Le Havre and Cherbourg. The post and the four firing blockhouses had been subjected to heavy allied bombing prior to D-Day.

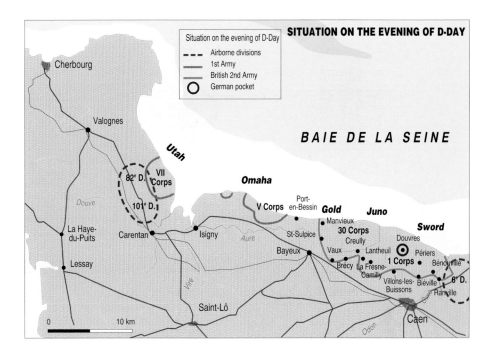

SITUATION ON THE EVENING OF D-DAY

Situation on the evening of D-Day
- - - Airborne divisions
——— 1st Army
——— British 2nd Army
○ German pocket

BAIE DE LA SEINE

" Chaos " battery on the cliff to the north of Longues–sur–Mer comprising a battery of 152 anti–ship artillery designed to fire out over the Baie de Seine. Partially destroyed by the air bombing raids, it managed to open fire on the allied ships before dawn on 6 June. The "Ajax" and the "Georges–Leygues" returned fire. One blockhouse out of four remained in tact. The battery was taken over by the British on the morning of the 7th. Its remains are still there today giving visitors an impression of the scale of the German fortifications.

A convoy of "Dukws" heading towards Utah Beach.
(R.H.A. document)

freedom of movement and communications as a result of the Allies' total control in the skies; and also the slow reaction time caused by an over-elaborate command structure.

Whereas Allied fighter aircraft made 10,536 sorties - not to mention 1,730 transport planes -, the Luftwaffe in the west only managed 319 sorties over the skies of France. It had a total 119 fighters, and a reserve of 33 battle-worthy fighters in the south of France. Any movement under the avalanche of bombs was slow and costly in lives and equipment. Telephone or radio communications between the command and the troops were sketchy.

The complex chain of command resulted in 21st Panzer hesitating, stepping and back-stepping throughout the day. Its counter-attack launched at 4 p.m. against troops that had disembarked 8 hours previously, and carried out with only a third of its resources, had succeeded in blocking access to Caen. Had an all-out counter-attack taken place in the morning, with 12th S.S. Panzer moving up quickly in reinforcement in the afternoon against the Allied

forces cornered on narrow, congested beaches - whilst at *Omaha*, the situation remained in the balance until early afternoon - the Germans could have considerably hampered the Allied operation. It would probably not have been sufficient to make it fail altogether. Indeed, on the Allied side, four years of effort, organisation of the command, the training of men and units, superior equipment, the intelligence service, special equipment design - all bore fruit and made up a force which would undoubtedly have reacted. This is indeed what happened in some areas on D-Day - regardless of the first hesitant efforts of some brand new troops and the theoretical arguments among the commanders. The concentration of resources and the common will of the men resulted in a rapidity of execution and a mastery of resources which it would be difficult to criticise.

A firm foothold on the Continent had been achieved: it remained to consolidate it in the face of opposition which, in view of the courage shown by the German troops, promised to be stubborn and intelligent.

Leaving Omaha Beach on D + 3.

(U.S.I.S. document)

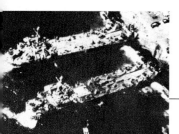

CHAPTER THIRTEEN

WIDENING
THE BEACHHEAD
(D + 1 TO D + 12 [7 TO 18 JUNE 1944])

By the evening of 6 June, D-Day, the battle of Normandy had begun; it was already apparent that it would be not be easy. A bridgehead had been established: it would now have to be widened. Caen, its airfield, and the open terrain near the town were objectives for the first day that were yet to be conquered: German resistance would be very powerful, and Caen would not fall into British hands until 8 July (D + 32). Cherbourg, the port the Allies needed to seize in order to insure the logistical support for the *Overlord* build-up aimed at the heart of Germany, would also require a long battle before its capture on 25 June (D + 20).

It was only once these objectives had been achieved that Eisenhower, Montgomery and Bradley would be able to envisage a break-out towards the ports of Brittany and north-eastern France. Extremely unfavourable weather conditions delayed the arrival of reinforcements and logistical supplies to the lodgement area. This delay, combined with dogged German resistance in the bocage, prevented, up till the end of July, the landing of the forces which Montgomery, still in command, required to end the war of attrition and move onto the offensive. Then came the break-out and exploitation ending on 20 August

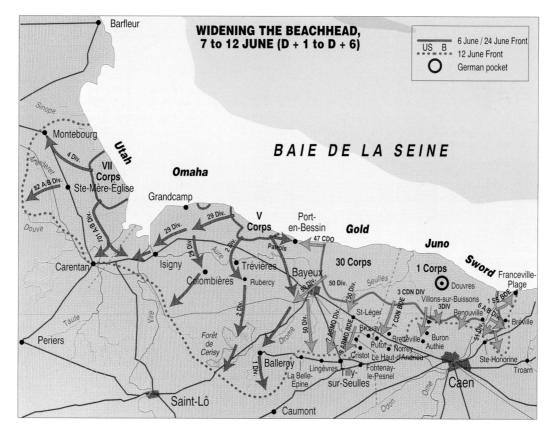

with the closing of the Falaise pocket, the end of the battle of Normandy - the road was then opened up to the Seine and Paris, liberated on 25 August, and on to northern and eastern France.

3 phases may be distinguished in the chaotic battles that followed the 6 June assault until 31 July, date of the start of the exploitation phase that would seal the fate of the German forces committed in Normandy:

– the widening of the beachhead (D + 1 to D + 12 [7 to 18 June]),

– the consolidation of the beachhead (D + 12 to D + 32 [18 June to 8 July]); battles for Cherbourg and Caen; the intervention of German reinforcements,

– the build-up and break-out (D + 32 to D + 55 [8 to 31 July]); the Cobra offensive.

These 3 phases will be dealt with briefly. They involved stubborn fighting between adversaries held in close contact along fronts which made no progress in muddy condi-

tions occasionally reminiscent of 1917.

As in the southern Cotentin, the bocage country in the small "Suisse Normande" area favoured the defenders. Armoured offensives, whether Allied attacks or German counter-attacks, could not be launched on any scale. The bad weather hampered the Allied landings required to bring extra men and supplies to the battle.

In France, Allied air supremacy and the Resistance - under the firm guidance of American, British and French paratroop squads, strengthened by arms drops - had a similar effect on the arrival of the German reserves.

During these two months, the Allies pegged away at the German defences, which were exhausted and had no hope of throwing them

Vierville Beach, D + 5.
(U.S.I.S. document)

7 June, German newspapers announce the invasion: "Invasion takes place on Moscow's orders". "Moscow's henchmen forced to start invasion".
(E.C.P.A. document)

L.S.T.s landing vehicles on the conquered beaches.
(R.H.A. document)

Landing vehicles and tanks on the beaches. Once the assault units (special engineers & infantry) had taken the beaches and de-mined the itineraries, the Landing Ship Tanks beached their tanks, vehicles and infantry.
(Photo - Archives des Armées)

back into the sea. The present narrative will only deal with the broad outline and the main tactical events.

By the end of July, the Allies were finally strong enough in their widened beachhead to move onto the offensive and, in a fourth extremely mobile phase, to encircle and almost entirely destroy the German forces engaged.

On the evening of 6 June, Hitler in eastern Prussia, von Rundstedt at Saint-Germain-en-Laye, and Rommel, back at his command post at La Roche-Guyon, were, for once, in agreement in their appreciation of the situation: the Normandy landing itself was a diversion, and the battle for the Cotentin peninsula was a diversion within a diversion. The apparent threat to Cherbourg was aimed at diverting attention away from the real objective, Caen and later the Seine, with a view to linking up with the main landing, in the Pas-de-Calais.

Accordingly, Fifteenth Army north of the Seine would be kept intact to face the main danger yet to come, guarding the V.I weapon launching sites, and barring the road to the Ruhr. A single battalion of Tiger tanks was all that could be taken from the Fifteenth Army forces and reserves, and as we shall see, they played an important role.

To face the Normandy landing, there were the forces of the Seventh Army, as well as von Rundstedt's strategic reserves which Hitler finally gave permission to engage.

General Dollman (Seventh Army at Le Mans) alerted his divisions garrisoned in Brittany, III Parachute Corps (General Meindl) with 3rd and 5th Parachute Divisions, 77th Division (Saint-Malo), 353rd Division (Morlaix), which were gradually committed between D and D + 6 (12 June).

Von Rundstedt's 5 available panzer divisions were also alerted. Two were within striking distance, Panzer Lehr (Bayerlein, a great figure of the *Afrikakorps*) and 12th S.S. Panzer (von Witt), of which a battlegroup commanded by Kurt Meyer only just made it to the area southeast of Caen on the evening of the 6; three were further afield: 17th S.S. Panzer Grenadier (without tanks, only armoured infantry and assault guns) close to Poitiers, 2nd S.S. Panzer Division Das Reich (S.S. *Obergruppenführer* Lammerding) in the Toulouse-Montauban area, 1st S.S. Panzerdivision *Leibstandarte* (T. Wisch) in Belgium, just back from the hard struggle in Russia.

Rommel directed that the diversion in the Cotentin be met by the divisions from Brittany, and that a panzer counter-attack be launched from Caen in order to throw the Canadians and British back into the sea. This had the following results:
- fierce infantry battles at the base of the Cotentin with VII U.S. Corps (Lieutenant-General Collins),
- hard tank battles in the sector north and west of Caen: German tanks of the 3 nearby panzer divisions against Dempsey's British and Canadian infantry and tanks, notably British 7th Armoured Division (Erskine),

- a gap in the centre into which General Marcks (LXXXIV Corps) had no reserves to commit until the arrival of S.S. panzer divisions coming very slowly from S.W. France.

In the sectors to the north and west of Caen, the commitment of panzer divisions would never be on the massive scale that Rommel wanted, namely a counter-attack all the way to the sea.

Caen. Aftermath of the bombing raids of June 1944.
(Photo - Delasalle.)

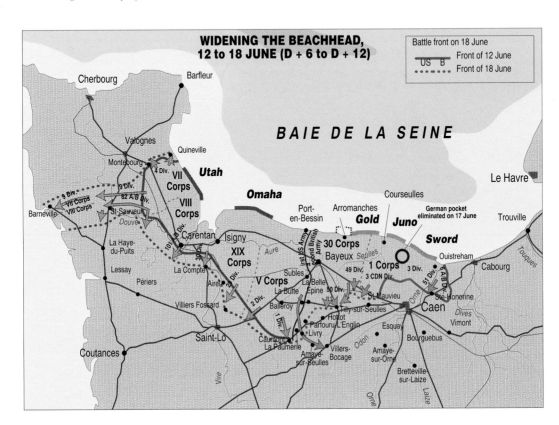

**Insignia
of the XXX British corps.**

**Insignia
of the 21st British Army Group.**

21st Panzer was, as we have seen, committed on the afternoon of 6 June on the Périers-Colleville ridge, north of Caen. On the 7, Feuchtinger attempted to rally the various elements of his 21st Panzer, and to counter-attack with reinforcements from Kurt Meyer's battle-group (12th S.S. Panzer) which arrived overnight with no fuel to spare. His defensive was hampered by an air attack on his force at sunrise, and by the commitment of Kurt Meyer against a Canadian attack towards Carpiquet. Meyer effectively repulsed this attack, but had committed his entire battlegroup in this defensive battle.

While these battles were unfolding to the north-west of Caen, the XXX British Corps, which had arrived outside Bayeux on D-Day, entered and liberated the town on 7 June, making it the first French town to be liberated.

On the coast, the British and Canadians finally linked up to establish a single bridgehead 20 miles long and 6 to 10 miles deep. The Canadians encountered only slight resistance from stragglers from 711th Division and the 12th S.S. Panzer reconnaissance battalion leading the way for Sepp Dietrich's I S.S. Panzer Corps.

With his two panzer divisions, 12th S.S. Panzer and Panzer Lehr, Dietrich had not a little difficulty in reaching the region S.W. of Caen. The panzer movements were continually subjected to Allied air bombardment. Rommel entrusted Geyr von Schweppenburg with the mission of attempting a massive counter-attack to the sea with his three panzer divisions. This attack came to nothing when Allied air superiority was brought to bear. Panzer Group West H.Q. was heavily bombed. Geyr von Schweppenburg was badly wounded and replaced by Sepp Dietrich. The two panzer divisions, 12th S.S. Panzer and Panzer Lehr, were engaged in hard defensive battles by British 7th Armoured Division around the village of Tilly.

A mobile front was set up ahead of the road from Vire to Caen which, being constantly strafed by the Allied planes, the Germans came to call *Jaborennstecke* or "fighter-bomber ally" (Jagdbomber or *Jabo* in German).

On 7 June, Eisenhower reviewed the situation with Montgomery and Bradley on board a destroyer. The situation at *Omaha* was still very worrying but would soon improve, the Germans for the moment having no reserves to engage in the centre to reinforce the 352nd Division which had already fought on D-Day.

The junction with the British was made at Port-en-Bessin to the east. By evening on 8 June the American beachhead at *Omaha* was 6 miles deep, linked to the British beachhead, and touched on the inundated zone at Isigny. Eisenhower and Bradley decided to try to join up the beachheads at *Utah* and *Omaha* before attempting to capture Cherbourg.

On 10 June (D + 4) Bradley, who had brought his H.Q. ashore on the 9 in the vicinity of the Pointe-du-Hoc, met Montgomery at Port-en-Bessin.

In the Cotentin peninsula, the airborne and seaborne troops continued to rally in a beach-head which extended 10 miles by 10 by the evening of 7 June, but remained isolated from the others, and their fate depended on the arrival of German reinforcements from Brittany. Like the panzer divisions moving up to Caen, these were considerably delayed by Allied bombardments.

On 12 June 101st Airborne managed to take Carentan after a hard battle: the link-up had been achieved. From Ouistreham in the east to Sainte-Mère-Eglise, the Allies had connected up a single beachhead 50 miles long and extending 6 to 18 miles inland - for the same day, through the gap that had opened up in the middle of the German battle array, U.S. 1st Division took the village of Caumont and the high ground 18 miles south of *Omaha* where they had come ashore. Attempting to exploit this advance, the British, immediately to the east, came out from Tilly towards Villers-Bocage on the Caen-Vire road, where an extremely costly battle was fought against the first German Tiger tanks to appear in Normandy, those of 101st S.S. Panzer Battalion. S.S. *Obersturmführer* Michael Wittmann, with his Tiger, obliterated a British armoured column in the village, clearing demonstrating the superiority of the Tiger with its matchless armour and gun.

By the evening of 12 June (D + 6), 16 divisions had disembarked in the beachhead, with 326,547 men accompanied by 54,186 vehicles and 104,428 tons of equipment.

The landings had fallen behind the planned schedule, not through any reaction from the German navy, but merely on account of the foul weather. By mid-May, in anticipation of the invasion, Donitz had tried to transfer a maxi-

mum number of U-boats, including 6 fitted with the Schnorkel, from the Baltic and Norway to the Bay of Biscay in order to combat *Overlord*. In the 6 first days, 12 out of 36 without Schnorkel were put out of action, and 24 others returned to port. Of the 6 with Schnorkel, none managed to reach the landing zone.

Pressure mines dropped in the sea by low-flying German aircraft were liable to cause a great deal of trouble. Rommel had requested for them to be dropped in advance: Donitz had refused lest the secret of their mechanism be discovered. They were first dropped in the Bay of the Seine in the night of 9-10 June. Some were found intact, and the Admiralty immediately found ways of dealing with this danger by imposing speed restrictions on shipping passing through infected waters.

In the night of 12-13 June the first V.- 1 weapons were launched against London; they reached a maximum 244 in the single night of 16 June.

At this same date, besides I S.S. Panzer Corps which as we have seen had been engaged west of Caen, German reserves from Brittany and central France had begun to be committed; on 8 June 353rd Division arrived from Morlaix, 3rd

Parachute Division was moved up from Brest to Saint-Lô, and 77th Division from Saint-Malo. Movements of divisions coming from central France were subjected to considerable delays due to the widespread damage to communications, and the harassment of troops on the move by Allied aircraft and the French Resistance carefully instructed by teams of *Jedburgh* parachutists in the most effective destructions to be carried out. Thus 17th S.S. Panzer Grenadier Division, alerted on 6 June at Poitiers, would not reach the Caumont area with its leading elements until 11 June. Rommel found himself obliged to commit elements as they arrived. Complete divisions could not be mustered before going into action. No armoured mass was ever brought together for a counter-attack. Thus 9th S.S. Panzer *Hohenstaufen* and 10th S.S. Panzer *Frundsberg* of II S.S. Panzer Corps on their way back from Poland took longer to cross France than to reach the Rhine from the Russian front, and would arrive piecemeal in Normandy from 25 June on. This record for slowness was broken by 2nd S.S. Panzer *Das Reich* (S.S. *Obergruppenfürher* which, after being alerted and sent on their way on the evening of 6 June, did not reach Noyers-Bocage (south of

Landing reinforcements on the conquered beaches. Allied air domination was such that it enabled the L.S.Ts to get right up to the beaches, like rows in a car park, to unload their load.
(R.H.A. document)

During the first days of the landing boats were deliberately scuppered to provide makeshift jetties. Photo depicts a "Marauder" from the US 9th Army and nine such ships being using as a protective jetty for transport approaching the beach.
(R.H.A. document)

Caen) with its leading elements until 28 June. Such was the irritation caused to the commanders at being constantly harassed by aircraft and the Resistance that this unit was responsible for the massacre at Oradour, perpetrated moreover after mixing up two villages with the same name.

Since 6 June Hitler intervened constantly in the battle. On 10 June he wrote: "Every man shall fight and fall where he stands." He left no room for manoeuvre to his generals for all their experience and courage, as displayed by General Marcks, commander of LXXXIV Corps, who was killed on 12 June, near Caumont as the town was being taken by U.S.1st Division.

This same 12 June, Rommel sent a report to

the German Supreme Command and to Hitler clearly describing the situation: "(...) the Army Group must content itself with forming a connected front between the Orne and the Vire (...) The Army Group is endeavouring to replace the panzer formations by infantry formations as soon as possible, and to re-form mobile reserves with them (...) The Army Group intends to switch its Schwerpunkt in the next few days to the area Carentan-Montebourg to annihilate the enemy there and avert the danger to Cherbourg (...)"

Pessimistically he summed up the situation: "The enemy is strengthening himself visibly on land under cover of highly superior air power. Our own air force and navy are not in a position to offer him appreciable opposition. Thus the strength of the enemy on land is increasing appreciably more quickly than our reserves can reach the front (...) Our position is becoming exceptionally difficult since the enemy can cripple the movement of our formations throughout the day, while he himself operates with quickly-moving formations and troops landing from the air. (...) The enemy has complete command of the air over the battle zone, and up to about 100 kilometres behind the front (...) Neither our flak nor the Luftwaffe seem capable of putting a stop to this crippling and destructive operation (...)"

Rommel was reduced to tenacious defence exploiting the bocage to the full against the

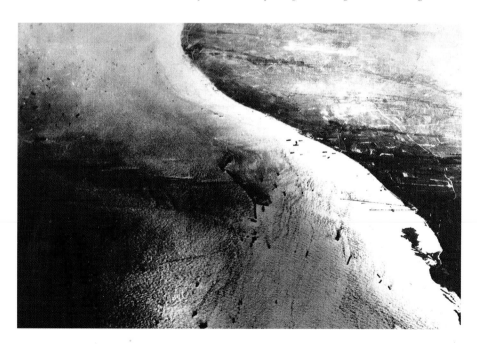

General view of the Port of Arromanches under construction. The photo depicts scuppered boats to provide protective sea walls and floating jetties leading to the lines.
(E.C.P.A. document)

14 June. General de Gaulle addressing the population of Grandcamp.
(E.C.P.A. document)

14 June. General de Gaulle reaches French soil at Courseulles and is welcomed at Bayeux, the first French town to be liberated (7 June).
(E.C.P.A. document)

Allied tanks. He did his best to plug the gaps on the front held from the north of Caen to the Cotentin, and in the peninsula, to protect Cherbourg, where, as he correctly anticipated, the Allies would make their next effort.

In the Cotentin, as soon as the junction had been made at Carentan, General Collins' VII U.S. Corps pushed on towards the port of Cherbourg. On 18 June U.S. 9th Division reached Barneville on the west coast of the peninsula, thus cutting the Cotentin in two.

On that same date, 18 June, the two artificial harbours at Saint-Laurent and Arromanches had been completed and were about to come into operation. Until then the landings had been made directly on the beaches and had been slow, all the more so since they had been considerably hampered by the bad weather. There were by now 20 divisions in the beachhead, and 24,500 tons of ammunition had been disembarked.

Since 9 June, airstrips had been set up on French soil where fighters could be based, thus facilitating the immediate tactical support of the front-line forces. In spite of the bad weather, Allied air activity never stopped, making the most of the slightest break in the clouds. During the first week from D-Day to D + 7 (6 to 13 June) the tactical air forces carried out close on 35,000 sorties.

On 18 June (D + 12), the Allied bridgehead had been sufficiently widened for Eisenhower and Montgomery to plan their next move: to consolidate the beachhead from the base of the Cotentin, and the high ground before Saint-Lô, to the ridges north of Caen and the mouth of the Orne; to go for Cherbourg in a swinging movement, whilst pressing against Caen in order to draw the enemy reserves, an effort that was already largely under way. The opening of the two synthetic ports would

4pm Place du Château, Bayeux, de Gaulle addresses a gathering of 2 000 French people surrounded by the local resistance fighters Mercader, Desprairies, Picot, Ligneul, military representatives that landed at Asnelles on 6 June, Maurice Schumann and Colonel Chandon as well as members of the Gouvernement légal de la France libérée set up at Bayeux.

now enable supplies to be brought to the battle-field at a sufficient rate to envisage offensive action.

The previous day, on 17 June, Hitler had sum-moned to his fortified Command post at Margi-val, near Soissons, his two field-marshals in the west, von Rundstedt and Rommel, for whom the interview was a disappointing affair. Von Rund-stedt confirmed what Rommel had written on the 12, namely that given the enemy's superior-ity in the air it was impossible to launch a counter-offensive. Rommel expressed doubts as to the possibility of containing the existing bridgehead. He suggested a withdrawal. Hitler remained calm, did not reply, but did not cancel his orders to fight yard by yard without retreat-ing, and to perish on the spot.

When Rommel dared to ask Hitler what he thought were their chances of continuing the war, he received the following reply: "That is a question that is not your responsibility. You will have to leave that to me."

Hitler spoke at length on the chances of suc-cess of the secret V. weapons and midget sub-marines, if only he could gain sufficient time through stubborn defence. He refused to use the V. weapons against the British ports of embarka-tion and against the Normandy beachhead since they were too inaccurate for such objectives. Elsewhere, that very day, a V.-1 had flown off-course, and instead of ending up in London, had landed right next to the Führer's bunker; and he was so alarmed by this incident that he can-celled the visit to Rommel's H.Q. that he was to have made the following day. The field-mar-shals, who had already left the bunker, would not see Hitler as had been arranged on June 18: they had got nothing out of this interview. Two days later, they received orders from Hitler to launch an offensive against the centre of the beachhead with II S.S. Panzer Corps recalled from Poland: the elite of the regime would have to succeed where the Wehrmacht had failed!

July 9. Members of the 1st battalion of the King's Own Scottish Borderers on patrol in the rue Saint–Pierre, Caen.

(R.H.A. document)

CHAPTER FOURTEEN

CONSOLIDATING THE BEACHHEAD

(D + 12 TO D + 32 [18 JUNE TO 8 JULY 1944])

the Battles for Cherbourg (25 JUNE [D + 20]) and Caen (8 JULY [D + 32])

SITUATION ON JUNE 30: Cherbourg has been in allied hands since 26 June and the forces of the American VII Corps (General Collins) responsible for its capture were able to be sent south between the VI and XIX Corps. To the south of Carentan, the Americans had still not been able to secure the area of the marshland and the flooded land. The US V Corps captured the dominant strategic location of Caumont to the south of Bayeux on 13 June. The British operation code-named "Epsom" took the form of a mounted salient on the River Odon between Villers-Bocage and Caen. To the north of Caen, the British have reached Périers rise where they were stopped by the German counter-attack by the 21st Panzer division on the afternoon of 6 June. To the east of the Orne, the beachhead creqted by the British 6th division on June 6 would be used to launch the attack in the direction of the plateaux to the south-east of Caen.

On 19 June (D + 12), after the bad weather that had delayed the logistical landings and the construction of the two artificial harbours, there came a storm that devastated the two harbours, which had only just been completed and placed out of range of inland shellfire by pushing back the front line. The harbour in the American sector off Saint-Laurent was damaged beyond repair. The one in the British sector at Arromanches would again become operational once repairs had been carried out. For several days the landings were seriously slowed down: whereas 25,000 tons of

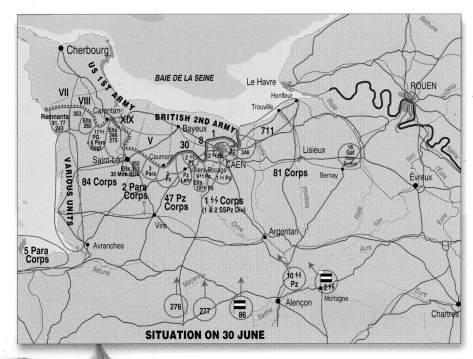

SITUATION ON 30 JUNE

D + 10 (16 June), two pre-fabricated artificial ports are put into place at Arromanches and Vierville. Each were designed to take a capacity of approximately 11 750 tons and 2 500 vehicles per day. The storm of 19 June (D + 13) put the one at Saint-Laurent out of action. The one at Arromanches, repaired after the storm was able to work at full capacity.
(R.H.A. document)

Powerful German defensive gun at Cherbourg.
(E.C.P.A. document)

ammunition were unloaded on 18 June, by the 20th this figure had dropped to 4,000. This had a tremendous impact on the tactical situation.

An attack planned to take place on 22 June to the west of Caen and code-named *Epsom* had to be postponed. The capture of Cherbourg took on a new urgency.

A new American corps, XIX Corps (General Corlett) had been introduced between VII and V Corps (which came ashore at *Utah* and *Omaha*) respectively) before Saint-L™. VII Corps (Lieutenant-General Collins) henceforth concentrated their efforts on attacking the north Cotentin with Cherbourg as their main objective.

Collins led his offensive with all the energy that he had deployed at Guadalcanal against the Japanese the previous year. He had the benefit of considerable reinforcements - 30 battalions in 12 days. Released from his responsibilities in

19 June (D + 13): the storm destroys the American artificial port which had just been built at Saint-Laurent putting it completely out of action. Some of its components will be used to repair the one at Arromanches also damaged by the storm.
(E.C.P.A. document)

THE ARTIFICIAL BRIDGE AT ARROMANCHES

The operation involved creating a vast artificial port off Arromanches near the centre of the landing sector by cordoning off a vast stretch of water and shelter it from the swell of the open sea by creating an artificial sea breaks.

The harbour was designed to take four unloading platforms connected to the land by a series of jetties. The entire installation was to be built in Great Britain and towed across the English Channel on the day after D-Day.

Mulberry port (official code name) with a surface area of approximately 1235 acres was an artificial harbour designed to handle approximately 6850 tonnes of merchandise per day. It needed to be operational within fifteen days of the landing and remain in operation until the beginning of autumn 1944. It was not fully operational until 19 July, the date on which the L.S.T. quay came into service.

In order to protect a stretch of water from the swell the decision was taken to sink support structures (known as Phoenix) weighing several thousands of tons parallel to the coast.

The Phoenixes could not be put into place straight away as seventeen ships had to be scuppered at sea first.

The *blockships* as they were known were designed to break the swell from the open sea.

Unloading quays were then installed in the resulting harbour comprising vast platforms measuring over 1 196 m2 designed to follow tidal movements by sliding along large piles on the sea bed.

Winston Churchill, who come up with the idea of the artificial port (later known as Winston harbour), wrote the following to Lord Mountbatten: "They must float up and down with the tide. A solution to the anchorage problem must be solved. Please send me the best one you can find. Please don't tell me it is impossible, the difficulties are patently obvious in themselves."

To reach the coast, a system of relatively flexible metal roads were laid over the floating steel or reinforced concrete casing supporting the bridge.

The harbour saw its best performance in the last week of July when Montgomery launched his attack on Caen. During the seven days in question traffic at Arromanches topped 136 000 tons, i,e, nearly 20 000 tons per day.

Above left:
Lord Mountbatten, who had the idea of the pre-fabricated floating ports, was quoted as saying: "Since we do not have a port, we shall bring our own."

Above right:
The floating breaks at the exit to the artificial harbour at Arromanches running between the floating quays and the beach. L.S.T.s were capable of unloading 60 vehicles in 30 minutes.. (E.C.P.A. document)

Opposite:
Photo of the artificial port in 1944.

the south where the American First Army went temporarily on the defensive, he lost no time attacking immediately after cutting the Cotentin in two on 18 June. At 3 a.m. on 19 June he took Montebourg by surprise.

The fortifications around Cherbourg were formidable, but von Schlieben, commanding the German troops in the north Cotentin, had only indifferent units and in insufficient numbers. He nevertheless opposed stout resistance to U.S. VII Corps whose 3 divisions stood before the outer defences of the city by the evening of the 20. On the 21, von Schlieben ignored an offer to surrender. The assault began. On 26 June all organised resistance in the city ceased. Von Schlieben was taken prisoner as was Admiral Hennecke, along with 30,000 men.

Sporadic resistance continued in the arsenal: all resistance in the north Cotentin finally ceased on 1 July.

Work was immediately started to restore the port installations. The first ship to enter Cherbourg harbour did so on 17 July.

With Cherbourg in Allied hands, the destruction of the bridgehead was no longer feasible. Without doubt von Rundstedt and Rommel

Ruined fortifications of Cherbourg. The structures remained unfinished at the time of the D–Day Normandy operation.
(R.H.A. document)

A DC–3 hospital truck sends up dust on a Royal Air Force inland airfield near Creully on July 1944.
(Canada public archives.)

recognised this and sought to reconstruct their armoured reserves and to launch a mobile delaying action. They were restrained both by Hitler's orders to stand fast and die on the spot and his belief in a second landing, in which they themselves were beginning to doubt. Although Hitler had been the first to have had the intuition that the main landing would take place in Normandy, this opinion was based on erroneous information and helped by the Allied deception plan that was still going on.

A German intelligence report wrote on 26 June - the day Cherbourg fell and there were 25 Allied divisions in the bridgehead, with another 15 waiting in England ready to land: "The enemy is employing 27 to 31 divisions in the bridgehead. (...) In England another 67 major formations are standing to, of which 57

at the very least can be employed for a large-scale operation."

Accordingly, the Fifteenth Army was hardly used and remained at the ready for a second invasion that failed to materialise.

It was then that the hard battles for Caen and the south of Caen commenced, battles that raged on until the end of July.

There has been much controversy as to whether or not operations carried out in this area conformed with the plans drawn up in England and presented on 15 May in London.

During the preparations, Montgomery had presented the following plan: "Second Army is to assault west of the River Orne, and to develop operations to the south and southeast in order to secure airfield sites and to protect the eastern flank of First U.S. Army while the latter is capturing Cherbourg. In its subsequent operations the Second Army will pivot on its left and offer a strong front against enemy movement towards the lodgement area from the east."

This statement seemed to restrict the action around Caen to the role of a defensive hinge. Some among the more offensive-minded thought that the open area south of Caen would be more favourable to a break-out than the bocage country spreading westwards from Caen to Avranches.

The question does not appear to have been resolved and in his operations report, Eisenhower simply writes: "In the east, we had been unable to break out towards the Seine and the enemy's concentration of his main power in the Caen sector had prevented us from securing the ground in that area we so badly needed. Nevertheless our plans were sufficiently flexible that we could take advantage of this enemy reaction by directing that the American forces smash out of the lodgement area in the west while the British and Canadians kept the Germans occupied in the east." And it was exactly what happened because General Eisenhower goes on to say that "incessant pressure by the second Army to contain the enemy's strength was therefore continued by Field-Marshal Montgomery during July". Simultaneously, the U.S. forces in the Cotentin proceeded to fight their way southwards, alongside those who had landed east of the Vire, to win ground for mounting the attack which was to break through the German defenses at the end of the month."

Montgomery's careful advance towards Caen and the south of Caen appeared too slow, especially to the airmen, who considered the capture of airstrips to be a vital objective; whereas successive thrusts and drawing the German reserves seemed to Montgomery to be an excellent way of unbalancing the German defences and favouring a break-out elsewhere.

The *Epsom* offensive towards the Orne west of Caen opened on the morning of 25 June: it had been delayed owing to the storms of 19 to 24 June that had hampered the landing of supplies, particularly ammunition. In this heavy bocage sector west of Carpiquet airport

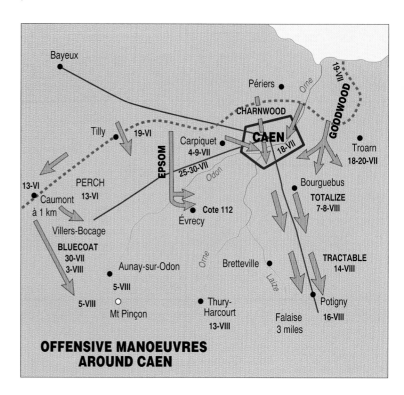

OFFENSIVE MANOEUVRES AROUND CAEN

astride the roads from Caen to Caumont and Villers-Bocage, 50th Division, 15th Scottish Division, 11th Armoured and British 43rd attacked. They encountered resistance from the panzers that General Dollman, commanding German Seventh Army, had mustered for lack of infantry.

Indeed, following the plan Hitler had set on 20 June, Rommel was attempting to gather a panzer column north of Vire whose mission would be to launch an attack towards Bayeux and Arromanches.

S.S. *Obergruppenführer* Hausser, commanding II S.S. Panzer Corps, comprising 9th and 10th S.S. Panzer Divisions, arrived on 23 June. These two divisions had stopped the Soviet offensive at Tarnopol in April. They had left Poland on 12 June, reached the French frontier on 16 June and since then had undertaken a laborious 375 mile march to Alençon, which they did not reach until 25 June. 1st S.S. Panzer had left Belgium and arrived in Normandy south of Caumont on 18 June via Paris - for everywhere else the bridges over the Seine had been destroyed. 2nd S.S. Panzer had great difficulty moving to Normandy, arriving on 28 June.

2nd Panzer (von Luttwitz) had been committed at Villers-Bocage since 18 June.

Montgomery had been informed of the arrival in Normandy of new armoured divisions, 1st, 9th and l0th S.S. Panzer and 2nd Panzer, through intelligence passed on by members of the Resistance and the air force. Their presence led to the conclusion that Rommel was about to mount an offensive. Montgomery wanted to forestall him and obtain the fall of Caen before Rommel could launch his offensive: this was his reason for wanting Operation *Epsom*.

For 5 days, a hardfought battle forced Dollman - who died of heart failure on 29 June - and Rommel to commit all their armoured reserves that they had just concentrated, including the famous II S.S. Panzer Corps under S.S. *Obergruppenführer* Hausser.

At the time of Dollman's death, the two field-marshals, von Rundstedt and Rommel, were at Berchtesgaden where Hitler had summoned them. To command Seventh Army Hitler appointed Hausser, the first S.S. officer to be raised to such a high rank, involving the command of Wehrmacht units.

Operation *Epsom* came to a halt on 29 June notably after fierce fighting on Hill 112, south of the river Odon, and again 2 miles from the Orne, that the British gave up trying to reach.

Hausser had to abandon the launch of one counter-offensive intended to cut off the Odon salient on account of the serious effects of the Allied aerial bombardment, favoured by the fine weather which had returned on the morning of the 29. From its arrival in Normandy, II S.S. Panzer Corps was subjected to enemy air superiority such as their campaign in Russia had not given them the slightest idea, but which was awaiting them as soon as they crossed the Rhine.

The interview with Hitler on 29 June was particularly disappointing for the two field-marshals. Rommel offered to lead a rearguard action back to the Seine and to relieve the armies in the south of France on a line Seine-Switzerland; failing which Seventh Army would be destroyed.

The British offensive had been stopped only at the cost of committing the entire strategic armoured reserve. Hitler would listen to no argument and restated his confidence in his secret weapons on condition that sufficient time was gained by holding ground at any price.

Hausser's final attempt against the British Odon salient failed on 1 July.

**Caen, July 1944:
the Eglise Saint-Pierre
after the victory, its steeple
blown off on 9 June by a " 406 "
from the cruiser
HMS " Rodney ".**
(E.C.P.A. document)

R.A.F. bombing raid providing tactical support by bombing road connections taken by enemy reinforcements. Photo depicts Villers–Bocage, 30 June 1944.
(I.W.M. document)

Marshall von Kuge, von Rundstedt's successor in July. He committed suicide on 17 August as a result of accusations of treason by the Führer.
(Bundes Archives, Koblenz.)

By the end of June German losses had increased to over 50,000 prisoners. The 7 panzer divisions committed had lost over 300 tanks.

On the evening of 1 July, Field-Marshal Keitel, whom von Rundstedt had just informed by telephone of the situation awaiting him on his return from Berchtesgaden, demanded: "What shall we do?" To which von Rundstedt replied: "Make peace, you fools. What else can you do?"

Immediately informed by Keitel, Hitler decided to replace von Rundstedt with the convalescent Field-Marshal von Kluge who was now available. After commanding an army in France and during the march on Moscow, between 1942 and 1943 von Kluge had led an effective defence in Russia at the head of Army Group Centre, a post he lost after an accident. He had a great reputation, and arrived on 4 July at Saint-Germain-en-Laye to take over from Field-Marshal von Rundstedt, who had nevertheless received a gracious letter from Hitler. Von Rundstedt's prestige remained high; a few months later, Hitler, aware of his value and the confidence that he inspired in his subordinates, restored him to his command in the west, before the battle of the Ardennes.

The *Epsom* attack, aimed at capturing Caen from the west, was stopped on 1 July; it had succeeded in drawing the bulk of the German tank forces. This was a substantial result because it made impossible the offensive ordered by Hitler towards Bayeux and Arromanches, for which purpose he had moved into Normandy II S.S. Panzer Corps (9th and 10th S.S. Panzer) from Poland and 1st S.S. Panzer from Belgium; but Caen had not fallen.

A Panzer IV overturned by a bomb outside Caen.

Caught between this Odon salient in the west and the pocket established by British 6th Airborne on D-Day east of the Orne, Caen found itself in a position which was deemed untenable from 1 July by the German commanders, namely: von Rundstedt due to be relieved by von Kluge, Rommel still in charge of Army Group B, and Eberbach who had taken over from the wounded Geyr von Schweppenburg. Eberbach, to the east of Seventh Army, gathered under his command 7 out of the 10 panzer divisions committed in Normandy. But Hitler refused to abandon Caen, even though it would have to be defended yard by yard.

On the evening of 7 July, in the first instance of tactical air support from the strategic forces, Air-Marshal Harris's Lancasters and Halifaxes dropped 2,500 tons of bombs on the northern suburbs of Caen. By morning on 8 July the converging British and Canadian 3rd Divisions managed to occupy the northern quarter of Caen, while the Germans of 12th S.S. Panzer and 272nd Division held onto the part of the city situated south of the Orne.

The capture of Cherbourg and occupation of the northern Cotentin on 26 and 30 June, the seizure of the northern sector of Caen on 8 July, marked the conquest of the original objectives set for Overlord and the end of the consolidation of the bridgehead. Behind the now unbroken line from Cap Carteret (on the west coast of the Cotentin) to Caen, the build-up for the offensive towards the interior of France would now be continued.

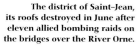

The district of Saint-Jean, its roofs destroyed in June after eleven allied bombing raids on the bridges over the River Orne.

Top: German grenadiers changing position. The woods and hedgerows of Le Cotentin peninsula stretched as far as the eye could see. Protected by high hedgerows, German grenadiers approach the landed Americans with caution armed with Panzerfaust anti–tank guns, automatic weapons and Mauser rifles.

Bottom: Battle of the hedgerows in La Manche.

CHAPTER FIFTEEN

THE BUILD-UP AND BREAKOUT

(D + 32 to D + 55 [8 to 31 July 1944])
The "Cobra" offensive (25 July)

At the beginning of July, it must be admitted that although Caen was finally in Allied hands, its outlets to the south were still held firmly by Eberbach's *Panzer Group West.*

Accordingly Montgomery prepared a new operation, Goodwood, to surround and bring about the fall of Caen from the east, from the "airborne bridgehead" established on D-Day between the Orne and Troarn. For this purpose he had 3 armoured divisions, 11th, 7th and Guards cross over to the eastern bank of the Orne under orders from VIII Corps commanded by General O'Connor. After a massive preliminary air bombardment, the objective of the attack, on 18 July, was to be the open terrain south and southwest of Caen towards Falaise.

Rommel, who had not failed to notice the British preparations, and who feared nothing worse than a thrust towards Falaise or Lisieux that would permit a break-out towards the Seine, had considerably strengthened the area south of Caen, the target of the British attack: he had brought in the 88 mm guns of 16th Air Defence Division from Holland, and the tanks of 1st and 12th S.S. Panzer and 21st Panzer.

Caen, cleared of Nazi troops once and for all on 18 July, lost 3000 civilian lives.

"Flak" gunners inspecting bullet-holes in a panel of an American bomber that they have just shot down.

On the afternoon of 17 July, Rommel was going to check the strength of the dispositions organised by Panzer Group West commander General Eberbach, now supervising the eastern section of the front, on the right of Seventh Army (at the end of July this command took the name of Fifth Panzer Army). On his return to his H.Q. at La Roche-Guyon, Rommel was attacked by Allied

fighters, and gravely injured. He was not replaced in his command, instead von Kluge combined both commands, West and Army Group B.

From 18 to 24 July, Operation *Goodwood* was met with stout resistance. The 36 Tigers played a vital role in this defensive on account of their superiority in armour and weaponry. British 11th Division lost 126 tanks in a single day, although suffering relatively few casualties, astonishingly few in fact. Caen was completely liberated, in ruins, and the plain of Caen had been cleared over a 5 mile belt around the city.

According to whether the objective of the operation was deemed to have been to clear the highways south of Caen, or to achieve a break-through towards Falaise, Goodwood was accounted a success or a failure. Within the

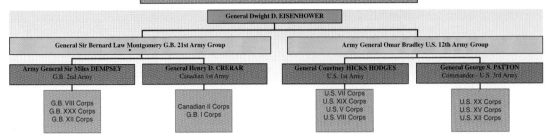

SUPREME HEADQUARTERS ALLIED EXPEDITIONARY FORCES
As of the beginning of August 1944

General Dwight D. EISENHOWER

General Sir Bernard Law Montgomery G.B. 21st Army Group | Army General Omar Bradley U.S. 12th Army Group

Army General Sir Miles DEMPSEY G.B. 2nd Army | General Henry D. CRERAR Canadian 1st Army | General Courtney HICKS HODGES U.S. 1st Army | General George S. PATTON Commander - U.S. 3rd Army

G.B. VIII Corps / G.B. XXX Corps / G.B. XII Corps | Canadian II Corps / G.B. I Corps | U.S. VII Corps / U.S. XIX Corps / U.S. V Corps / U.S. VIII Corps | U.S. XX Corps / U.S. XV Corps / U.S. XII Corps

Allied High Command, some, like Tedder and Leigh-Mallory, and perhaps Eisenhower himself, expected better results for two reasons. In the operational directive of 13 July from General Dempsey to General O'Connor figured the name of Falaise, which could therefore appear to have been the objective of the attack. By temperament Eisenhower wanted a general offensive attitude along the entire front from east to west, now that the logistical support for the battle had been achieved. Montgomery, commander-in-chief of the ground forces, considered himself satisfied with the result obtained, since it opened up to him the roads south of Caen and had drawn the bulk of the German armour to the east, leaving the situation along the west of the front so much easier for exploitation by Bradley and Operation *Cobra*, planned for 20 July.

Accordingly Eisenhower reviewed the situation with Bradley and Montgomery on 19 July.

Indeed with July two-thirds over, it appeared to the Allied command to be stagnating and to have made less progress than had been hoped.

At the beginning of July, Bradley, freed of the worry of capturing Cherbourg, transferred all his forces southwards, i.e. 4 Army Corps numbering 14 divisions along a 48 mile line between the west coast of the Cotentin, south of Saint-Sauveur, and Caumont. He confronted the bocage country which by nature particularly suited the defence of the fifteen, certainly sorely tried and weakened, but experienced, divisions of German LXXXIV Corps. Since the death of Marcks, killed at Caumont, this corps had been commanded by Farmbacher, who was dismissed after the fall of Cherbourg. It was taken over by von Choltitz, just back from Russia, himself under orders from Hausser, who had arrived from Poland to be promptly placed by Hitler in charge of Seventh Army.

British divisions: Guards, Desert rats and 2nd AD, three divisions making up the British VIII Army Corps, Goodwood 18/07 then Bluecoat 31/7.

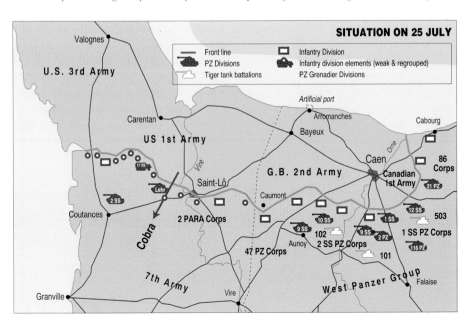

SITUATION ON 25 JULY

SITUATION ON 25 JULY (line held at the time of the "Cobra" attack):

The 7th Army (Hausser) have come up against the U.S. 1st Army (Bradley) and the West Panzergroup (Eberbach) – the 2nd British Army (Dempsey). The US 3rd Army would be created shortly afterwards and break through the lines past Avranches. General Bradley subsequently took over as commander of the 12th U.S. Army Group (1st Army and Patton's 3rd army). The Panzergroup was renamed the 5th Armed Panzer in August. August 1st: up against 36 allied divisions, the thirty German divisions resisted with varying degrees of strength.

End of July 1944: Saint-Lô in ruins after tough combats which ended in it being taken by the Americans on 19 July.
(R.H.A. document)

Throughout the first part of July, U.S. First Army had fought hard battles to wear down German resistance: this was the "battle of the hedgerows". The very bad weather added to the difficulties of the advance. Between 1 July and 25 July, U.S. First Army managed with some difficulty to extricate itself from the marshy region around Carentan that cut the front in two. It captured La Haie-du-Puits on 8 July after a battle lasting 7 days around this town. It gained roughly 6 miles: on 25 July, the line held from Caumont, the pivot, included Saint-Lô conquered on 19 July, and ran along the north side of the Périers-Lessay road solidly held by von Choltitz. The latter had lined up his divisions for the yard by yard defensive ordered by Hitler, including the Panzer Lehr Division which had been fighting without interruption since 8 June, initially close to Caen. His only reserves were, north of Coutances, 2nd S.S. Panzer, which had arrived from Toulouse at the end of June.

Bradley had planned to launch the offensive, code-named *Cobra*, on 20 July, with the help of newly landed reinforcements. But disruption of the artificial harbours at Saint-Laurent and Arromanches made it necessary to continue the landings on the beaches. In spite of these delays, thanks especially to intensive utilisation of Utah and Omaha beaches, in the space of 7 weeks the Allies managed to bring ashore 36 divisions, plus numerous air and ground follow-up and support units, altogether 1,566,000 men, 332,000 vehicles and 1,500,000 tons of equipment and ammunitions.

By 20 July, resources were allocated to launching the offensive. Cobra was planned for this date, but was postponed until the 25 in view of the poor weather conditions.

This long month of July could well therefore appear to the Allies as a "gray" month, with a war of attrition in the west that proved costly in human lives, supplies coming in through the beachhead behind schedule as a result of weather and sea conditions, and inadequate progress in the Caen area.

On 19 July, Eisenhower was doubly disappointed after conferring with Bradley and Montgomery. Bradley had informed him that the Cobra attack planned for the following day would have to be postponed because of the weather. And Montgomery was quite satisfied with the result of the Goodwood armoured attack to the south-east of Caen although it struck him as something of a hollow success.

Without losing his customary composure, Eisenhower passed his impression on to Churchill. On 20 July Churchill visited Montgomery who pleaded that his hinge tactics were sound and expressed optimism with regard to the coming operations.

This crisis within the Allied command was soon forgotten in the face of the sequence of events of the next few days.

Meanwhile, on 20 July an attempt was made on Hitler's life. It does not seem to have had any direct consequences on the German fighting behaviour in Normandy: the troops continued to fight well, and even very well. At the command level, it increased Hitler's mistrust of his military commanders – particularly those coming from the ranks of the nobility, and there were many of these –, and thereby further aggravated existing ambiguities in the command structure. Hitler came increasingly to rely on his own followers, the S.S. units and commanders. The already difficult relations between the army and the S.S. became even worse. On the other hand, the failure of the attack, added to Roosevelt's stated demand for unconditional surrender, would deter those German commanders more concerned about the future of Germany than their commitment towards Hitler from looking to the Allies for a compromise solution that would both save Germany and protect Europe from communism. Moreover any attempts that were made in this direction, – which having no bearing on the actual fighting, have no place here –, received a blunt refusal from the Allies.

Henceforth Hitler's power was greater than ever. All-out war with no hope was the way forward for all, the believers, who were in the majority, as well as those who no longer believed in Hitler and wanted to save Germany.

In spite of offensives launched in the east (the Soviet offensive had commenced on 23 June to the north of the Pripet marshes) and the west, in spite of the Allies' continued strategic bombing campaign (partly diverted however to the flying bomb sites directed against London), the Germans still had vast resources. During the second quarter of 1944, the German factories delivered 4,545 single-engine aircraft, against 2,545 lost in combat and almost as many destroyed on the ground or damaged. Similarly, during the period from May to July, the Wehrmacht received 2,313 tanks from the factories while it lost some 1,730. Transportation posed more problems than actual production due to the threatening oil shortage,

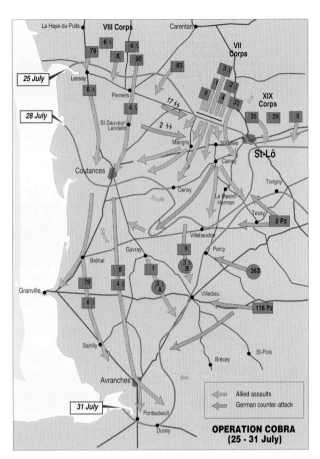

OPERATION « COBRA » (25 TO 31 JULY)

The capture of Avranches on 30 July and the bridge at Pontaubault marked the end of "Cobra" and the beginning of the allied breakthrough towards Brittany and the Loire which ended with the surrounding of the German 7th and 5th armies on 8 July.

OPERATION COBRA (25 - 31 July)

disrupted communications, and the need to replace qualified staff. From 6 June to 23 July, Seventh Army and Panzer Group West lost 116,863 men with only 10,078 coming out from the training centres; a mere 20 tanks replaced the 3 or 4 hundred that had been knocked out. What Bradley's offensive, soon to be extended on the left flank by the British, first towards Mont Pinçon dominating the centre of the Allied front line, then in the southern sector of Caen, was mainly up against was the fanatical bravery of the German soldiers under experienced commanders.

Bradley hoped to launch *Cobra* on 20 July. On the strength of his experience of the "battle of the hedgerows" he improvised an effective device to be adapted onto his equipment: the front of many Sherman tanks were fitted with sharp steel blades; such tanks, known as "Rhinos", could cut through the hedge and bank,

General Collins, Chief of the US VII army Corps in June 1944.
(U.S. Army document)

advance without losing speed, keep firing and open the way up for other tanks and infantry. Strategic bombers would precede the break-out with a carpet of bombs over a rectangle 5 miles long by 1,5 miles deep. Postponed from the 20 to the 24, Cobra was again put off at the last moment to the 25, owing to bad weather, although the bombers had already flown on the morning of the 24 and dropped their bombs in poor visibility, partly on the American troops. On the morning of the 25, the "carpet" of bombs was laid by 2,250 aircraft including 1,500 strategic bombers. Heavy bombers used only 50 kg (110 lb) bombs, since in Caen larger size bombs had had the disadvantage of producing craters which the British troops found to be impassable. In spite of a few bomb-aiming errors due to a misunderstanding between U.S. First Army and U.S. VIII Air Force, the Carpet Bombing made the Cobra break-out a success. German LXXXIV Corps was badly mauled, including the Panzer Lehr Division, in reserve close to Marigny, 10 miles from Saint-Lô, caught right in the firing-line and the main effort of the U.S. First Army spearheaded by the ever offensive-minded Major-General Collins's VII Corps. The German infantry defended each foot of ground and every hedge; to provide liaison between the American infantry and their

General Hodges who was to take over the command of the US 1st Army from Bradley on 13 August 1944.
(U.S. Army document)

A light Stuart reconnaissance tank leading the "Cobra" thrust.
(National Archives U.S.A.)

tactical support aircraft, rapid signalling methods had been devised which proved as effective as the "Rhinos".

The Allied attack spread out on either side of the initial area while the spearhead U.S. 2nd Tank Division reached the Tessy-Bréhal road on the 27 and made a broad sweep around Coutances which fell on the 28.

German LXXXIV Corps had disintegrated and its commander, von Choltitz, whose withdrawal had displeased Hitler, was replaced by General Elfeld.

Immediately to the east, on 28 July, Montgomery ordered Operation Bluecoat with Dempsey to cover the flank whilst U.S. First Army advanced and an attack towards Vire to be launched by VIII Corps on 30 July. Bény-Bocage and Vire were reached on 1 August, and Mont Pinçon was taken on 4 August.

Immediately after 28 July, the Cobra offensive took on a dimension that had been unhoped for when it was launched on the 25. U.S. 4th Armoured pushed boldly through the gap opened up at Coutances; on the evening of 30 July it reached Avranches, 30 miles further south, managing to seize the bridge at Pontaubault that opened up the road to Brittany and the Loire at Nantes. The break-out had been achieved.

At that same moment, Bradley handed over the command of U.S. First Army to General Hodges, until then his deputy, and took command of American 12th Army Group, comprising U.S. First and Third Armies. This Third Army was set up under the command of General Patton, with the more western divisions of First Army, recently disembarked armoured divisions, and VIII Corps (General Middleton) that had just broken through at Coutances, Avranches and Pontaubault.

The final phase of the battle of Normandy could now commence, with the exploitation of the break-out by U.S. First Army at Avranches.

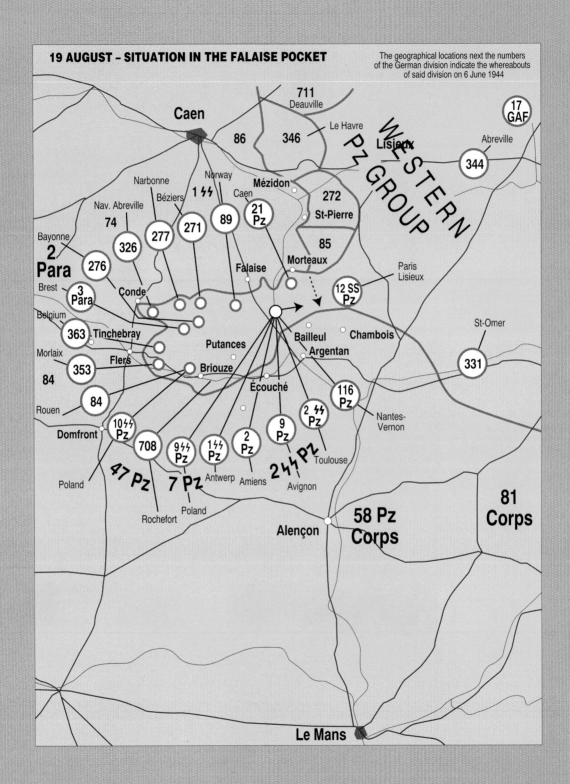

19 AUGUST – SITUATION IN THE FALAISE POCKET

The geographical locations next the numbers of the German division indicate the whereabouts of said division on 6 June 1944

Culmination of the Battle of Normandy. The pocket was closed on 20 August.

CHAPTER SIXTEEN

EEXPLOITING THE BREAK-OUT

The German counter-attack at Mortain (7 August)
Destruction of the German army in the Falaise
pocket (15 to 20 August)
End of the Battle of Normandy

Rommel.

If the situation in mid-July appeared to the Allied command to fall short of expectations built up after the successful landing, the German command nevertheless found it to be an extremely dangerous one. Before his injury and evacuation, Rommel was pessimistic in a report he sent to Hitler. He remained confident in the defensive system that he had put in place around Caen, but he wrote: "Within a measurable time, the enemy will succeed in breaking through our thinly held front, especially that of Seventh Army, and in thrusting deep into France. (...) The force is fighting heroically everywhere, but the unequal struggle is nearing its end. In my opinion, it is necessary to draw the appropriate conclusion from this situation." This report was forwarded to Hitler on 22 July by von Kluge who enclosed his own personal message. The enemy had total supremacy in the air, in the face of which no strategy of

opposition was possible: "I came here with the fixed determination of making effective your order to stand fast at any price. But when one has seen by experience that this price must be paid in the slow but sure annihilation of the force (...) anxiety about the immediate future of this front is only too well justified. (...) In spite of the intense efforts, the moment has drawn near when this front, already so heavily strained, will break. (...)"

This letter showed how radically von Kluge's situation had changed in less than 20 days, from being hitherto ever victorious, even when on the defensive in Russia. Having arrived at Saint-Germain on 4 July sure of success, he was now convinced of the necessity to yield ground and the methodical withdrawal of the forces under him as being the only way to save them.

Nevertheless Hitler reiterated his order to hold firm at any price and would continue to

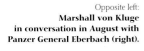

Opposite left:
**Marshall von Kluge
in conversation in August with
Panzer General Eberbach (right).**

Opposite right:
**August 1944. General Patton
chief of the U.S. 3rd Army,
General Bradley, chief
of the 12th US Army Group,
General Montgomery,
Chief of the British 21st Army
Group at the HQ of the 21st
Army Group.**
(R.H.A. document)

do so in the course of the hard days ahead during the rapid advance of Patton's Third Army from the bridges at Avranches and Pontaubault.

In the face of all logic, in 72 hours Patton got 7 divisions across the only bridge that he held. Rennes was reached on 4 August; U.S. 4th Armoured raced to Vannes, and 6th Armoured reached Brest on 7 August and lay siege to the city, which held out until 18 September.

On Bradley's order, U.S. VII Corps seized Mortain on 2 August to give some breathing space to the breakthrough at Avranches. On 3 August Bradley ordered Patton to leave the minimum necessary force in Brittany and carry his main effort eastwards. Montgomery, who had held on to the mission to coordinate 2 army groups, his own and Bradley's, confirmed the sweeping move to the German rear towards Paris, to force the enemy back to the Seine.

On 2 August, Warlimont, sent by Hitler and Jodl, brought von Kluge the order to restore the broken front. For von Kluge, while the Americans had taken Mortain and the British spread the pressure to Vire and kept II S.S. Panzer Corps occupied, there was no question of closing the gap opened up at Avranches. He suggested withdrawing his entire force to the Seine under the cover of a group of mobile divisions provided by Seventh Army on the western and

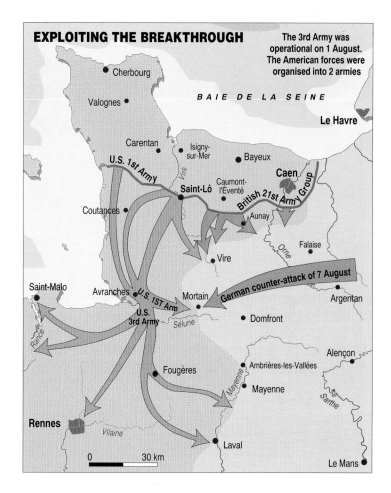

EXPLOITING THE BREAKTHROUGH

The 3rd Army was operational on 1 August. The American forces were organised into 2 armies

Beginning of August 1944: American troops on the move near Coutances at the start of the breakthrough.
(E.C.P.A. document)

Film reporters the accompanied the American units everywhere they went.
(U.S.I.S. document)

The American blood bank for European operating theatres arriving in England by hospital DC–3s in Thermos containers.
(U.S.I.S. document)

The bridge at Pontaubault over the River Selune. Patton managed to get seven divisions across in 72 hours.
(R.H.A. document)

underlined the dire risk for the American Third Army in the event of the German counter-attack reaching its objective in spite of the defence of Mortain by the U.S. First Army and British operations towards Vire and Mont Pinçon. The importance attached by Hitler to the success of this counter-attack was clear from a resumption of activity on 6 August of German aircraft recalled from the eastern front to support von Kluge.

southern flanks. Hitler replied on 4 August with a formal order to launch a counter-offensive against Mortain and Avranches to the sea with 8 of the 9 panzer divisions in Normandy. Convinced of the futility of this attack, as indeed was Hausser although a faithful Nazi, von Kluge did his best to assemble the panzers from the divisions spread along the front north of Caen at Vire, and heavily engaged against the British. He planned to launch the assault as early as possible, during the night of 6 to 7 August.

Whilst these preparations were proceeding, Third U.S. Army XV Corps (Haislip) carried out an outflanking manoeuvre from the south, approaching Le Mans on 6 August.

VIII Corps was left alone to operate in Brittany. The new XII and XX Corps prepared to pivot eastwards.

First British Army was to pursue its effort south of Caen towards Falaise and Argentan where the link-up was to be made, to the rear of the German Fifth and Seventh Armies, with the Third Army corps heading due north from Le Mans via Alençon.

In assembling his panzers at Mortain, von Kluge's preparations did not go unnoticed. They

At dawn on 7 August, the attack was launched by XLVII Panzer Corps (General von Funk), combining all the armour that von Kluge could lay his hands on. 2nd S.S. Panzer retook Mortain but hardly got any further: 1st S.S. Panzer and 116th Panzer hardly made any headway at all. Only 2nd Panzer under the excellent General von Luttwitz managed to advance as far as Juvigny and Le Mesnil-Adelée nearly 10 miles from its start line. But Avranches was still another 12 miles off. The tanks lacked infantry to hold the terrain: they were subjected to attacks from the Allied air force. The inevitable withdrawal followed and Mortain was retaken by the Americans.

In any case there was no way of the Germans avoiding being encircled. Bradley, alerted from the 5 by von Kluge's preparations in gathering

the armour from the northern front with a view to attacking Mortain, informed Eisenhower of the threat to Patton's rear and on the difficulties of getting fuel and ammunition supplies to the 4 corps that had pursued beyond Avranches in order to outflank the German armies from the south. On 8 August Eisenhower told him to continue his manoeuvre and not to worry about supplies to Patton, which he was ready to bring in by air if the German forces succeeded in cutting Third Army's lifeline at Avranches.

From then on, the fate of the German Seventh and Fifth armies was sealed. The outcome was only decided after an incredible tangle lasting 12 days, the stages of which must now be put in order.

To the north, when the British and American armies linked up, Mont Pinçon fell on 6

Between Sartilly & Avranches. Reconnaissance Stuart tanks from the 3rd Army encounter columns of prisoners from the 7th army en route to processing centres then England or the USA.
(U.S.I.S. document)

Lieutenant-Colonel Rouvillois from the 12th Armoured Cavalry surveys the progress of his armoured unit from the top of his tank.
(E.C.P.A. document)

Astonishment quickly gives way to joy as Normandy inhabitants realise that the G.I.s participating with honour in the liberation of Normandy (followed shortly afterwards by Paris) are actually French soldiers wearing American uniforms.
(U.S.I.S. document)

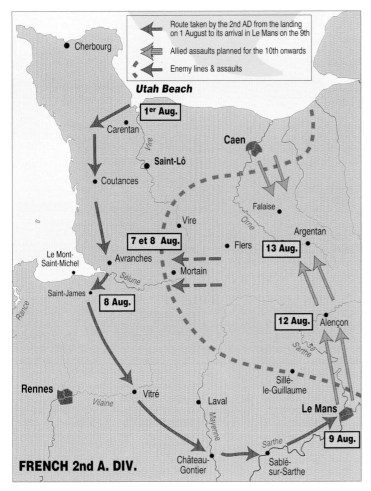

Route taken by the 2nd AD from the landing on 1 August to its arrival in Le Mans on the 9th

Allied assaults planned for the 10th onwards

Enemy lines & assaults

Utah Beach

1er Aug.

Cherbourg

Carentan

Caen

Saint-Lô

Coutances

Falaise

Vire

7 et 8 Aug.

Flers

Argentan

13 Aug.

Le Mont-Saint-Michel

Avranches

Mortain

Saint-James

8 Aug.

12 Aug. Alençon

Rennes

Vitré

Laval

Sillé-le-Guillaume

Le Mans

9 Aug.

FRENCH 2nd A. DIV.

Château-Gontier

Sablé-sur-Sarthe

General F. Morgan's directives to Cossac delivered by the C.C.S.s in April 1943 stipulated that a French division should be included in the landing force. The French government chose the 2nd A.D. (commanded by General Leclerc) for this assignment. The 2nd A.D. joined England in several detachments from Easter onwards (April 9th). The French 2nd A.D. landed at Utah on 1 August. It was incorporated into the XV Corps of the 3rd Army (Patton), reached the breach at Avranches and was bombed near Saint-James on 8 August before going on to Le Mans via Vitre, Château-Gontier, Sable. It captured Alençon on 10 August and reached Argentan on the 12th. One of its groups participated in the operation to the close off the pocket on 19 and 20 August, joining up with the 1st Polish A.D. at Mont-Ormel. It was then sent on to Paris which it liberated on 25 August.

12th armoured infantry of General Leclerc's 2nd A.D. landing at Saint-Martin-de-Varreville, Utah Beach on 1 August 1944.
(E.C.P.A. document)

The French army sets foot on French soil once more four years after the defeat of June 1940.
(U.S.I.S. document)

To the right, U.S. 5th Armoured reached Argentan the same day. Bradley ordered Patton to stop there and await the arrival of forces of British First Army coming from the north.

Meanwhile, south of Caen, the Canadian First Army, comprising Canadian II Corps and British I Corps under General Crerar had accounted for the sector east of the Orne. It went back onto the offensive on 7 August; code-named "Totalise", this new attack astride the Caen-Falaise road began at midnight on 7 August. The Canadian general commanding the operation was hoping that a night assault would bring the element of surprise

August, and Vire was taken on the 7. This increased the pressure on the Mortain pocket.

To the south, spurred on by Eisenhower's assurance given on the 8 to supply by air if necessary, Third Army continued to advance.

On 10 August XV Corps (Haislip) emerged from Le Mans facing north. It encountered stalwart but improvised resistance from 9th Panzer newly arrived from Avignon.

French 2nd Division (General Leclerc) landed at Utah on 1 August as part of XV Corps, took Alençon on 11 August and Ecouché on the 12.

that had been lacking in previous operations south of Caen. However, 12th S.S. Panzer was thoroughly familiar with the terrain on which it had been fighting since 8 June, and the Germans put up stout resistance. "*Totalise*" had to be halted on 9 August 6 miles short of Falaise.

A new attack, "*Tractable*", was launched down the same road and in turn came to a halt 2 1/2 miles outside Falaise in the face of stubborn resistance from the German panzers, the Tigers in particular. The number of Tigers was dwindling, but neutralising or destroying just one of them was quite an operation every time.

Falaise was not taken, in ruins, until 16 August. The gap eastwards out of the pocket in which the German Fifth and Seventh Armies were trapped was down to a mere 12 miles wide.

The pocket itself was getting narrower every day under the attacks of the American, Canadian and British divisions and the incessant aerial bombardment. But the German divisions put up admirable resistance: soldiers and commanders alike showed courage such as deserved a better fate.

On 15 August Field-Marshal von Kluge himself arranged an appointment with Eberbach, commanding 5th Panzer Army, inside the pocket, at Nécy, 2 miles S.W. of Falaise. His escort was attacked by the air force, and his radio car was destroyed. He failed to join Eberbach, and was cut off for a whole day, and his Chief of Staff Blumentritt could not get through to him to inform him that Hitler wanted to speak to him.

Von Kluge returned to his H.Q. alone on the morning of the 16, by which time Hitler had already decided to relieve him of his command. Hitler's mistrust since 20 July was such that he suspected him of having attempted to make contact with the Allies during his day's absence in order to negotiate.

A M8 Greyhound from the 5th US A.D. stops for refreshment southern La Manche.

(U.S.I.S. document)

Operating as mobile fortresses supported by small combat groups of S.S. grenadiers, heavy Tiger tanks from the V Panzer army waged impressive rear guard fights against the Canadian 1st Army and could only be stopped by Typhoon rocket fire. Photo depicts the Tiger belonging to crack Panzer commander Michael Wittman blown up when its ammunition exploded after a Typhoon-Rocket attack at Cintheaux on the Plaine de Caen (8 August 1944).

Generals Bradley, Gerow, Eisenhower and Collins. General Gerow was in charge of the U.S. V Corps. General Collins was in charge of the U.S. VII Corps which landed at Utah on 6 June and captured Cherbourg on the 27th, broke through the lines (Cobra attack) between Périers and Saint-Lô on 25 July and moved into Mortain on 2 August.

(R.H.A. document)

Meanwhile, the pocket became a furnace, a real "cauldron" from which the German forces attempted to escape on 19 and 20 August, leaving their equipment behind.

The corridor was closed at Trun and Chambois on the 19 when the Canadians and the Poles arriving from Falaise joined up with the Americans and French of XV Corps coming from the south.

A few stragglers also managed to escape on the 20, with the help of a counter-attack launched from the outside by elements of 2nd and 9th S.S. Panzer Divisions who had been evacuated from the pocket on 17 August.

In his operations report, Eisenhower summarises this final phase of the Normandy campaign: "In the pocket, the enemy's strategy was to line the southern lip through Argentan with his armor to defend against the American forces, as he extricated what he could through the gap, while a strong defensive barrier against the Canadians was established with the 12th SS

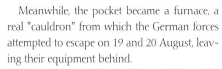

Polish men from the 1st Polish A.D. of General Stanislaw Maczek who landed at Arromanches from 14 July onwards. They had not forgotten their objective for returning to the continent: Warsaw via Normandy and Berlin, but were never to reach it as the Soviets were to get there first.

(Polish Institute.)

Panzer and 21st Panzer Divisions at Falaise. By this means, resisting fiercely, he managed to hold open the jaws of our pincers long enough to enable a portion of his forces to escape. As usual, he concentrated on saving his armor and left the bulk of his infantry to their fate - a subject of bitter comment by prisoners from the latter units who fell into our hands. A considerable part of the 1st SS Panzer, 2nd SS Panzer, 9th SS Panzer, 12th SS Panzer, Panzer Lehr, and 2nd Panzer, 9th Panzer, and 116th Panzer Divisions managed thus to get away; but the 326th, 353rd, 363rd, 271st, 276th, 277th, 89th, and part of the 331st Infantry Divisions, with some of the 21st SS Panzer and 10th Panzer Divisions, were trapped. Those armored forces which did escape however, only did so at the cost of losing a great proportion of their equipment.

Until 17th August, there was a steady seep eastwards through the gap, but then came a convulsive surge to get out on the part of all ranks; and the orderliness with which the retreat had hitherto been carried out collapsed suddenly.

On 16 August, U.S. Third Army was released from its mission against the pocket and relieved by elements of U.S. First Army.

It threw all its army corps in exploration in the open terrain towards the Seine. Orleans was reached on 17 August, Fontainebleau on the 20. After taking Alençon and Argentan, XV Corps (Haislip) managed to establish a bridgehead on the Seine at Vernon on 19 August. Army Group B H.Q. at La Roche-Guyon that von Kluge had just left, was caught in their fire.

Thus the battle of Normandy came to an end on 20 August (D + 75).

The cost of this battle to the German army is difficult to assess exactly. General Zimmermann, a

Advanced American first aid post used to treat all men indiscriminately. Photo depicts German parachutists accepting aid from the nurses.
(U.S.I.S. document)

Fleure, 13 August 1944. General Leclerc in conversation with a tank crew from the 501st R.C.C.
(E.C.P.A. document)

– 400,000 men including 200,000 prisoners;
– 1 300 tanks;
– 20 000 trucks;
– 500 guns;
– plus about forty divisions committed and eliminated (43 by Montgomery's count).

In his operations report, Eisenhower concludes his account of the battle of Normandy making the following points: "In assessing the reasons for victory, one must take into account not only the achievements in the field but the care and foresight which was applied to the preparations before D Day.

It was to the meticulous care in planning and preparation by my staff, supported resolutely in all important aspects by the Combined Chiefs of Staff, that we owed such essential factors as the degree of surprise achieved in our landings, the excellence and sufficiency of our amphibious equipment, and the superb organization which lay behind the

4 August 1944. Destruction of a German convoy attempting to escape from the " cauldron " to Chambois.
(R.H.A. document)

Right:
Montgomery awards a medal to an English soldier.
(I.W.M. document)

member of panzer group west staff, gave the following casualty figures in men:
– 6 June   to 25 June: 43 070
         to 15 July: 97 000
         to 7 August: 148 075
         to 14 August: 158 930

Taking into account the theoretical number of men per division, the number of divisions committed, the weakened state of some of these, the number of men that made their escape from the "cauldron" at Falaise on their own and empty-handed, counts of equipment recovered in the weeks and months after 20 August, the following seems a reasonable estimate of German losses:

miraculous achievements of our supply and maintenance services. While it is true that we had hoped that the tactical developments of the first few days would yield us the territory south and southeast of Caen, so suitable for the construction of necessary airfields and for exploitation of our strength in armor, the fact remains that in the broad strategic development we attained our anticipated line of D plus 90 two weeks prior to that date and in substantial accordance with our planned strategic program. The greatest factor of all, however, lay in the fighting qualities of the soldiers, sailors and airmen of the United Nations".

Reims, 7 May. The landing opened the way for victory in Europe. Photo taken after the Germans had signed an unconditional surrender. Photo depicts: Russian Major–General J.Susloparoff, the British General F.Morgan, Captain H.C.Butcher, Shaef's aide de camp, General Eisenhower, Supreme Commander, General A.Tedder, Deputy Supreme Commander, Admiral Burrough, Naval Commander.

(R.H.A. document)

CHAPTER SEVENTEEN

CONCLUSIONS

STRATEGIC AND TACTICAL ASSESSMENT

The conclusions presented in this brief synthesis of the unfolding of the battle of Normandy are categorised in four sections:

I - Equipment
II - Human
III - Tactical
IV - Strategic

I - EQUIPMENT

Tiger I tank used by two organic heavy tank battalions from the 1st and 2nd Panzerkorps.
(E.C.P.A. document)

The scale of resources committed by the Allies brings four points to mind.

a) The resources made available for the greatest ever amphibious operation were on a huge scale. The organisation and coordination with which they were used were remarkable. It is idle to dwell on this point, which has already been made abundantly clear by many authors as well as in above-quoted figures.

Some significant figures deserve to be added to those already quoted.

On the evening of 11 June, i.e. after 6 days, while no airfield or port was yet available, the

Tiger II tank used by the 503 Panzer Abteilung. Tiger tanks in action in Normandy played an essential role resisting the British and Canadian offensives around Caen in particular. They were responsible for destroying the large majority of allied tanks in this sector. Deployed non-stop, they were countered by allied air raids and very few were to escape from the "cauldron" of Falaise. None appears to have made it back across the Seine.
(E.C.P.A. document)

beachhead contained the following, brought ashore on the beaches:
– 326 547 men;
– 54 186 vehicles;
– 104 428 tons of supplies and equipment).

This result was obtained through outstanding organisation and preparation over a 3 year period, naval superiority, and lastly, most of all, absolute air supremacy gradually achieved since 1941.

"Only on 12 June", wrote Eisenhower, "did [the Germans] react in any considerable strength when a mass onslaught was made on French airfields by 1,448 Fortresses and Liberators of the U.S. Eight Air Force. (...) Weekly Allied losses average only about 1% of the aircraft employed" .

As regards resources, the Germans were outmatched but knew how to make the best use of the equipment they had and exploited the terrain favourable to the defender with great competence. Two weapons were superior to their Allied counterparts: the 88 mm anti-aircraft guns used as an anti-tank gun, and better still, the Tiger tanks, which also carried the 88 gun and whose armour was impenetrable. The hundred or so Tigers Mark I and II committed in Normandy played a decisive defensive role,

notably around Caen, and, during the final phase, in holding open of the corridor of exfiltration from the Argentan-Falaise pocket on the northern flank. S.S. Obersturmführer Wittmann, who was killed whilst commanding the I S.S. Panzer Corps heavy tank battalion close to Caen on 7 August, was credited with a personal tally of 138 tanks destroyed. Between 10 July and 20 August the heavy tank battalion of II S.S. Panzer Corps, under S.S. Obersturmführer Weiss, knocked out 227 Allied tanks. Almost all the Tigers were destroyed under fire from Allied aircraft. A few, perhaps 4 to 6, managed to escape the cauldron and reach the Bernay area. But not one of them made it across the Seine.

b) However huge the resources involved, the final outcome of the war was really decided by the value of the fighting troops, on "human commitment in the moment of truth". There are endless examples of this that one might quote:

– the 3-man crew of the two submarines that waited for 48 hours on the sea bed in front of the beaches,

– the paratroops jumping in the dark into the unknown, whatever the amount of information and rehearsal they had had,

– the crews of the 350 mine-sweepers slipping through the night to clear the path ahead for the armada of 5,000 vessels,

– the men in the D.D. tanks coming ashore amid raging seas,

– the sapper caught under fire during mine-clearing operations,

– the infantryman who, when trapped on the narrow stretch mined beach between the sea and enemy fire, followed the example of General Cotta and stood up and got things moving at *Omaha*, late on the morning of 6 June.

Nowadays when reliance on advanced technology dominates military thinking, this situation observed in June 1944 is still worth pondering on.

General Sir Alan Brooke, General Eisenhower, Winston Churchill, Prime Minister.
(E.C.P.A. document)

In the chaos of war, would not the computer be more quickly "destabilised"‑ to use an in-word of that time – than man; who may find himself all the more naked now for having previously been so heavily equipped.

c) With hindsight, in view of the serious difficulties encountered in spite of the huge resources thrown into the battle, the Allied command was justified in accepting the unavoidable delays required for producing and assembling them on English soil.

The existence of a powerful naval artillery capability in direct support was of considerable assistance in resolving the crisis on *Omaha beach*.

The success of the amphibious assault at *Utah* and its effective exploitation was only possible in conjunction with the dropping of 17,000 paratroops requiring the existence of a transport convoy of 1,662 aircraft and 512 gliders, as well as an adequate escort for these.

The slow advance during the first few days proved the wisdom of the decision to increase the amphibious assault forces from 3 to 5 divisions, and to delay *Overlord* as a result.

It was imperative to win the battle of the Atlantic in order to ship two million men over to England; however it was only in the second half of 1943 that the Allies began to overcome the German U-boats.

In July 1943, 37 German U-boats were sunk; in August 1943, 20; and 15 in each of the four first months of 1944. It was this gradual victory that brought the tonnage sunk on the Atlantic crossing (and in convoys taking supplies to the U.S.S.R. via Murmansk), down from 600,000 tons/month in January 1943 to 120,000 tons/month in the first quarter of 1944.

Similarly, as we have seen, it was only after 4 years of effort that the vital air supremacy needed to compensate for the unavoidable numerical inferiority of ground troops during the landing, was achieved.

d) All these resources had to be brought together because no risk of failure could be taken: the opening of the second front was a prerequisite for crushing Germany. The landing simply had to succeed. The Allies, particularly the British in their island at the edge of the Continent, were like a hunter who has only one cartridge in his gun: he must shoot to kill. If the landing was thrown back into the sea – something which the German Panzers could realistically hope to do – building up a new force would have given Hitler the time he needed to produce new submarines, mines still in the research stage, secret and perhaps even nuclear weapons. Nothing short of occupying

General Maczek presenting Chiefs of Staff of his 1st Polish Armoured Division to Montgomery.
(Polish Institute.)

the heart of Germany could put an end to Hitler's power: something Russia could not do. In July 1944, Germany, which had been under intense bombardment from the air for a year, had faced threats on land from the east, west and south, which experienced its one and only internal convulsion with the plot against Hitler, nevertheless managed to turn out 1,600 tanks and 2,700 new or renovated fighter planes from her factories.

11 - HUMAN

The scale of the German defeat was massive in both human and material terms.

In Normandy, there was no surrender and no capitulation: the rapid closing of the "cauldron of Falaise" by Haislip's U.S. XV Corps allowed the American Third Army, then held up with the pocket, to resume its drive towards the Seine with success such as would have wide-ranging consequences on the strategic level.

It is difficult to make any accurate estimation of forces committed and losses on the German side. About forty divisions of uneven quality and varied composition, including ten armoured, had been committed: to these were added many supporting units, permanent coastal batteries, and independent formations (three Tiger tank battalions and 88 mm anti-aircraft batteries, with remarkable anti-tank capabilities). Nothing of this survived except burnt-out wreckage. Credit must indeed be given to the 20,000 or so men who managed to escape from the Falaise pocket on 19 and 20 August in the midst of American, British, Canadian, Polish and French formations, although without their equipment (25 tanks and 60 guns that did not get across the Seine).

The Canadian Cemetery at Reviers. It is just possible to catch a glimpse of Bernières or "Juno" beach, site of the 3rd division and the 2nd Canadian armoured brigade landings, behind the trees on the northern boundary of the cemetery site.

The British Cemetery at Ranville situated in the centre of the parachute zone of General Gale's 6th airborne division. Large numbers of British parachutists were laid to rest at the foot of the church.

Right:
The American Cemetery at Saint–Laurent–Vierville containing nearly 10 000 graves is situated on the road which runs along, and overlooks, Omaha Beach.
(Photo – French air force.)

Below:
La Cambe Cemetery where 20 000 German soldier killed during the landing operations were laid to rest is one of the three large German cemeteries in Normandy. There other two are at Huisnes and Orglandes.

Thus the battle was about as costly as the huge pockets on the eastern front: 450,000 losses including 200,000 killed, and in equipment: 1,500 tanks, 2,000 guns and 20,000 vehicles.

Casualties among the generals were very high, although some divisional commanders managed to escape from the pocket together with a few hundred men:

– army, corps and divisional commanders killed or taken prisoner 20
– army commanders wounded (Rommel, Geyr von Schweppenburg, Hausser) 3
– divisions eliminated or out of action, around 35

Thus losses were comparable to those of the Russian offensives on the eastern front: but this was altogether a different battle on the strategic and tactical levels.

**Utah Beach.
The Musée du Débarquement Américain can be seen in the foreground t the right.**
(Photo – French air force.)

III - TACTICAL

The battle of Normandy was a great tactical victory for the Allies, in four ways:

a) the conditions in which the invasion was organised created tactical surprise, no little achievement given the Germans' certain expectation of a landing. We have related above how this surprise was achieved, and how uncertainly was kept up as to the nature of the landing: whether it was the main effort or merely a diversion.

b) Another aspect was specific to the particular case of the battle following on from a seaborne landing. On coming ashore, the forces immediately enter the fray and some start from 0, with no space in which to move. Creating a lodgement takes time, leaving the enemy time to bring up reinforcements with at least equal if not greater speed than the landing itself. This is what happened with the arrival of tank reinforcements from the centre of France to the Caen area, and the arrival of infantry reinforcements from Brittany and the west to Saint-Lô.

Thus the German forces settled into a continuous front with a troop density two and a half times greater than on the eastern front.

On the other hand supplies getting through to the Allied forces passed through the bottleneck of the beaches and the artificial harbours whose output was disturbed by the gales of 19-22 June, and remained below expected levels at a crucial stage in the build-up.

Consequences inherent to the landing operation were unavoidable; these were:

– a disappointing deadlock from 12 June to 20 July, falling short of planned results, especially as regards Caen and Saint-Malo;

– a ruinously hard-fought battle for the Allies, from 6 June to 20 July, with 177,000 fighting troops put out of action:

 • killed: 17 700
 • missing: 13 500
 • wounded: 85 830 ;

– the difficulty in widening the lodgement area; the great tactical victory was to have succeeded in doing so.

The manner in which the initiative was recovered has been the subject of much controversy; to some, it appeared that Montgomery had merely executed his plan; for others, it was the consequence of the failure to take Caen. Whatever the causes, the result was a concentration of German panzers around Caen, and a lopsided deployment of the German forces: the opportunity was intelligently seized to break out in the west and to recover a manoeuvring capability.

This tactical success was not therefore due to superior numbers, as had been the case on the eastern front (3 to 1, whereas in Normandy the odds were of 1.25 to 1), but to an imbalance in the distribution of the German forces.

c) gas was not used: the beachheads would have been rather vulnerable.

Although Hitler had large stocks of gas, he abandoned any thoughts of using it because, according to some, he himself had been a victim of it twice during the First World War, according to some. He was probably deterred by Roosevelt's declaration that he would use the same methods in reprisal against German cities and industrial concentrations, which were much more vulnerable.

The hamlet and port of Arromanches viewed from the cliff at Manvieux. Above Arromanches, the rise of Saint–Côme marking the centre of the landing zone separates Arromanches from the beaches at Asnelles–le–Hamel ("Gold"). Photo clearly depicts the orientation table and a monumental statue of the Virgin.
(Photo O.F.)

At Margival on 17 June, Hitler, von Rundstedt and Rommel contemplated attacking the Allied zone with the V.- I which had first been tested five days previously. This plan was dropped owing to the inaccuracy of these weapons.

d) The progress of the battle was modified by some fortunate tactical initiatives taken by the Allied command.

We have just mentioned how Montgomery gained a lodgement, the basic difficulty of any amphibious operation being precisely that no such space exists at the outset. Among others taken at the time, the following decisions should be noted:

– the decision taken by Bradley to launch the Cobra attack with massive "square" support from the strategic air force;

– the timely decision to seize Caumont on 12 June, a salient that served as a hinge for further offensive manoeuvres in the bocage;

– Bradley's decision of 3 August to leave as few of his men as possible in Brittany and make an all-out eastward drive to Le Mans and beyond;

– finally the vital decision taken by Eisenhower on 8 August to give Patton's army a free rein and supply it if necessary by air, in the event of the German attack at Mortain reaching the sea and cutting Patton off.

Set against these judicious moves, particularly the last one, a controversial decision was taken by Bradley and confirmed by Eisenhower on 12 August, to stop Patton and Haislip at Argentan, and not to go north beyond the boundary separating the U.S. and British Army Groups of Bradley and Montgomery. This decision meant that the Falaise pocket was sealed later and less tightly than would otherwise have been the case, thus allowing some 20,000 Germans who should not have escaped to do so, including some top quality German generals such as Hausser, Meindl, von Luttwitz, etc. who lived to fight another day in the Ardennes.

This decision can doubtless be explained by issues at Inter–Allied command level, and in no way undermines the strategic and tactical success of the battle.

Emblems from General Bradley's car.

IV - NORMANDY: The strategic victory of the war

a) The battle of Normandy thus drew to a close. It had begun with an unprecedented achievement of considerable strategic value, being a vital prerequisite for an end to the conflict. It was continued with a hard-fought battle causing some unforeseen delays. It finished 15 days earlier than Eisenhower had estimated (D + 75 instead of D + 90), and opened the way into the heart of Germany.

Of course this perspective took longer to achieve than it looked as though it might: but this had nothing to do with the battle that had just been fought. The Russian offensive timed to take place in conjunction with Overlord came to a halt outside Warsaw and the slow-down of the Allied offensive in the west due to logistical problems gave the German command some breathing space. The quality of the German soldier enabled this respite to be put to good use with a recovery in October that extended the war for a further winter.

b) The battle of Normandy was the essential and decisive strategic victory of World War II.

From 1933, the Axis gradually built up around Germany with Japan and Italy had gone from success to success over a 9 year period.

The loss of world equilibrium that began in June 1940 had continued to worsen until May 1942. Midway was the first setback for the Axis, and however uncertain it may have at first appeared to the Americans, this victory was the first strategic battle of the war. Further tactical successes, whether defensive or offensive, would follow this defensive turning point of the war: El-Alamein, Stalingrad, Tunis, Sicily, Kursk, Orel, etc.

But in order to re-establish the world balance, it was necessary to carry the offensive battle to the heart of Germany, the birthplace of Nazi totalitarianism.

Nothing short of a landing on the mainland of Europe could make this possible, and a difficult enterprise it was.

A perilous enterprise, a prerequisite for the liberation of Europe, and the end of the conflict and the holocausts, Overlord had to succeed at the first attempt: this was achieved.

POSTFACE

I had my personal share in the events related in the foregoing pages, modestly carrying out orders.

I felt the emotion of it all. My memories have no place here: perhaps, God willing, some day I shall write them up from my contemporary notes. However I should just like to mention one here, a particularly moving memory in connection with the battle of Normandy.

At that time I belonged to the staff of General Leclerc, the commander of French 2nd Armoured Division. This division was then heading home across the Atlantic from North Africa in an L.S.T., and some were already back in England. I myself had arrived, and was billeted with the H.Q. in Yorkshire. One morning I went to liase with the American staff, to whom we were responsible - G.4 (4th bureau) Tusa at Knutford.

I was handed a document, a small one: it represented, the horizontal stretch of terrain between the Seine and the Loire from Brest to the Rhine, with communications from the lower Normandy coast to the Seine at Rouen, south of Paris and eastern France.

This gave me a shock. The whole forthcoming operation came to me in a flash. Returning to H.Q. I hastened to show General Leclerc where the landing was obviously going to take place.

The hope I had caressed for the last 4 years of once again stepping on the soil of France was suddenly a dream no longer: it was taking shape. That small map gave life to it - I still have it pasted onto the page of my diary at the date on which I was given it: 23 May 1944, a fortnight before D-Day.

This map showed where the landing was to take place as well as the plan of subsequent operations. It shows that Paris was not included in the advance but was to be outflanked to the north and south. This is indeed what began to happen around 15-20 August 1944. The Seine was crossed at Mantes and Montereau by the American 1st and 3rd Armies, whilst the leading elements heading towards Paris had still barely reached Dreux and Chartres. It was then that, by request of General De Gaulle, Eisenhower sent the French 2nd Armoured Division and 4th US Infantry to Paris.

The purpose of this personal account is to stimulate reflection on the issues surrounding the Battle of Normandy:

THE FIGHTING SPIRIT & ACTION OF THE COMBATANTS

The fighting spirit and action of the combatants was profoundly influenced by the ideology and faith they respectively espoused.

Normandy was an arena which saw a clash between combatants driven by different convictions.

America was almost drawn into the war unwittingly, its conviction gradually growing that it was the right thing to do and that it needed to win it in order to defend both its own freedom and that of other countries and in order to re-establish world peace.

Such a belief did not come automatically. It was one that had to be nurtured, as illustrated by films shown at the time with titles such as "Why we are fighting". The result was not fanatical fervour rather a steadfast belief that it was the right course of action to take and undeniable, calm courage.

The German soldiers' belief in Nazi ideals undoubtedly had a major influence on their fighting spirit and action. To illustrate this issue I would like to quote the opinions of four different German generals.

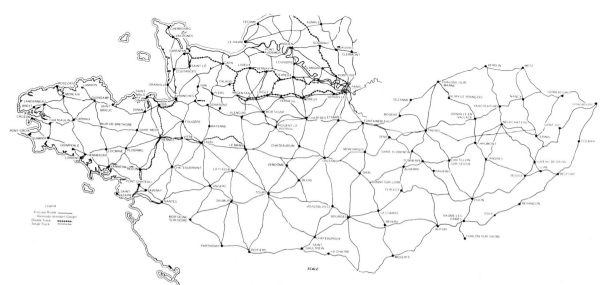

Map handed to Capitain Compagnon from General Leclerc's headquarters on 23 may 1944 by the American authorities (4th logistics bureau) directing the 2nd A.D. in England.

This is what General Blumentritt, von Rundstedt's Chief of Staff, had to say about the German soldiers: "They did not bear up under artillery fire as well as our troops had done in the other war. Generally speaking, the German .infantry was less proficient than in 1914-1918. Rank and file soldiers espoused personal opinions and were not sufficiently obedient. The rapid influx of men in the army, increasing numbers, meant a drop in quality standards since there was not enough time to discipline recruits through training".

General Elfeldt, von Choltitz's successor in charge of the LXXXIV Corps, expressed a different opinion: "National Socialism was both positive and negative in terms of discipline. Relations between officers and soldiers were significantly better than in 1914-1918 which was conducive to obedience. Such an improvement can be attributed to the new concept of discipline inculcated in the Reischwehr after our experience in the last war and the effects of National Socialism which blurred distinctions between officers and men. Simple soldiers showed more initiative and were more given to thinking than those in the Great War."

This statement appears to be somewhat surprising in view of the "mass movement" instinct inculcated by National Socialism. Elfeldt explained this by attributing it "to scouting instruction received by soldiers who had been in Hitler Youth organisations".

Another German general made the following statement: "The effects of National Socialism were multi-faceted. On the one hand it made things difficult for us as a result of eroding our personal authority. On the other hand, it fostered strong sense of patriotism which was more deeply held than in 1914-1918 and fostered a more vigorous fighting spirit than before. This resulted in stronger levels of fighting, even in during military setbacks."

General Westphal wrote: "After the Declaration of Casablanca stating that only unconditional surrender would be acceptable to the Allies, even those were aware of the real situation saw no other alternative than to fight to the bitter end".

The offensive courage of the Americans motivated by a belief in the freedom of democracy and the defensive courage of the Germans motivated by a patriotic fervour inspired by totalitarianism were remarkable indeed. The debate is still very much alive and merits further consideration.

NEUTRALITY & AID VIS–A–VIS WARRING COUNTRIES

Neutrality and aid vis-à-vis warring countries via the sale of arms are very much contemporary issues with the latter now a world-wide phenomenon.

Between 1940 and the end of 1941 there were several instances of so-called neutral powers aiding warring countries. The first such instance was the provision of assistance by the United States (neutral) to England which was at war. The American attitude was typified by a certain concern for efficiency, coupled with cautious prudence to comply with international laws and to avoid taking any courses of action which would shock domestic opinion.

The aid provided by England to the U.S.S.R., also war-related and that provided by the United States, while still purportedly neutral, directly or via the British are two more examples which merit reflection.

A thorough examination of this issue would be of significant educational value today.

THE LEGACY OF THE "WAR MAP"

The effects of the Normandy landings and subsequent operations combined with successive tactical offensives on the Russian front contributed to the military situation prevailing after the war had ended.

The "War Map" resulting from the aftermath is by and large similar to the current situation, i.e. in which Europe is divided in two.

Yalta and Potsdam were primarily opportunities to take stock of the situation rather than negotiation. Will such lessons be heeded in the context of current and future international and local conflicts? We have reason to believe so. The issue warrants reflection.

Over fifty years have passed. Two generations have reached maturity and entered active life. They sometimes forget to remember gratefully the Allies to whom they owe the freedom they have always known; especially several million Americans who came from afar.

To combat this forgetfulness and negligence, I shall quote a young soldier at the time in General Leclerc's 2nd Armoured, Jacques Salbaing, who took part in the campaign in France from Normandy to Germany. In November 1944, in the muddy, cold and wet Lorraine, he attacked a village in a battle which followed on from the capture of Baccarat and was a prelude to the victorious march on Strasbourg. He provides the following simple account:

"Meanwhile, elements of US 79th Division in the initial assault wave, got into position; one company even came right up against us. A few soldiers took the opportunity to make a short stop and have a bite to eat before setting off again, ever calm, to meet their destiny; trudging along with weapons at the ready. Day broke with overcast skies, and large snowflakes brought visibility down to under 30 yards or so. But they melted on the ground which got steadily muddier. Watching them go by, we could not help sincerely feeling for these fellow infantrymen on their way to battle, usually with no glory and no glamour, suffering from the damp cold, with soaking feet heavy with mud, and laden with kit and ammunition they had to carry for miles... They attacked in successive waves, commanded by their officers who, with a mere gesture, raising their arm, not shouting or saying a word, set them off on what seemed like an exercise against a notional enemy. The operation took place in front of our eyes, for they were attacking on a grassy slope which dropped down towards Barbas and Blamont. Mown down by the German machine-guns, they would stop, even retreating in places, but started up again irresistibly with the same calmness, the same cool determination. Boys from Arkansas, Oklahoma or California had come to be killed and suffer on what was for them foreign soil."

" Future generations must never lose sight of the fact that it is thanks to the Americans that their country was liberated. We all too easily forget, often for reasons of political dogma carefully organised by unscrupulous politicians contaminated by an outmoded ideology. You have to have seen what our American friends did during this war to be able to speak of it admiringly and without flattery."

Jacques Salbaing, "Ardeur et réflexion", Editions La Pensée Universelle.

APPENDICES

THE BATTLE OF THE ATLANTIC

Winning the freedom to sail the Atlantic, and then the Channel, was vital in order to bring American forces and supplies over to England, and then land them in France. The fierceness of the struggle may be illustrated by some figures:

- **GERMAN SUBMARINES:**
  - Stock and shipbuilding:
    - Existing in September 1939: 50 comprising
      - 1/3 operational in the action zone,
      - 1/3 under maintenance-repair,
      - 1/3 on their way to the action zone.
    - Existing in January 1943 (at the time of the Casablanca conference): 400 including 200 in the Atlantic.
    - U-boats built from 1939 to 1945: approximately 1,000.
  - Losses:
    - Sunk at sea during the war: .... 630 }
    - Sunk in port during the war: ....123 } 753
    - Destroyed during the year 1942:   82
      - during the "black month" of May 1943: .. 41
                                   in July 1943: . . . 37
                                   in Aug. 1943: .. 20
      - during the first 4 months of 1944
        (prior to *Overlord*) :   60

- **ALLIED TONNAGES SUNK:**
  - September 1939 to July 1942: .... 2 800 000 tons
  - In November 1942: .... 750 000 tons
  - In January 1943
    (at the time of the Casablanca conference) : ...... 567 000 tons
  - In February 1943: .... 380 000 tons

- In March 1943: .... 590 000 tons
- In August 1943: .... 86 000 tons

Statistics of Allied losses in tons sunk, as well as U-boats destroyed, situate the "turning point" in the battle of the Atlantic in the Allies' favour in May 1943. This was the consequence of decisions taken at Casablanca in January 1943, the effect of which began to be felt 5 months later.
But the battle raged on right until the launching of Overlord. During the 4 first months of 1944, i.e. prior to *Overlord*, Allied losses averaged roughly 120,000 tons per month. But from the second half of l943 on, for every ship sunk, at least 4 were built and took to the sea.

Special mention must be made of American shipping sunk in American waters in the 5 months that followed Germany's declaration of war on the United States. A mere 6 German U-boats operating off the east coast of the United States managed to achieve some remarkable results against merchant ships coming out of port, clearly silhouetted against the illuminated shore, and with protection from the merchant navy only and negligible air cover.
- January 1942: .... 200,000 tons sunk
- March 1942: .... 354,000 tons sunk
- May 1942: .... 452,000 tons sunk
                   (41 41 ships sunk by 6 German U-boats).

From the end of 1942, protection allowed by the production of escorts and reconnaissance planes brought an end to these dreadful losses. But Allied, especially American, losses during the first half of 1942 considerably delayed the movements to England, and also the U.S.S.R., as planned by Churchill and Roosevelt during the Arcadia conference in Washington (December 1941) immediately after Pearl Harbour.

DAMAGE TO GERMAN INDUSTRY CAUSED BY ALLIED BOMBING IN 1943

It is hard to assess the effect of the Allied bombing raids, which had been British up to the end of 1941, and then a joint Anglo-American operation from 1942 on.
German industrial production kept up its peace-time rate until 1942; it therefore had plenty of room for growth, which was exploited only upon Speer's arrival as Minister of Armaments and War Production in 1942. Speer devised a plan to step up production that in fact only came into effect after 1943 when losses and damages sustained at Stalingrad convinced Hitler of the need to increase production. This expansion thus coincided with the gradually increasing number of Allied bombing raids carried out in the course of 1943 in accordance with the decisions reached at Casablanca in January.
German industrial output thus saw considerable growth in 1942 and 1943 compared with negligible progress during the first two years of the war. And in December 1943 (at the time of Eisenhower's designation as Supreme

Commander of *Overlord* after the Tehran conference that brought together Churchill, Stalin and Roosevelt), Speer planned on further industrial growth that would however be limited by a shortage of steel. In 1943, Speer managed to raise the monthly steel production from 2,400,000 to over 3 million tons. But this figure was close to the limit created by the blockade, and was only a fifth of Allied capacity.
Nevertheless, by the end of 1943, arms and ammunition production was one and a half times that of 1942, and the German army was better equipped than in June 1941 during the attack on Russia, particularly both in the quantity and quality of their tanks.
The armoured force of 4,500 tanks in January 1941 passed the 11,000 mark in January 1942, with Panthers and Tigers gradually replacing medium and light tanks. In January 1943 there were 72 Tigers and Panthers; in January 1944 1,823 were operational and 375 more were coming off the production line each month.

The following table shows monthly production at various times:

	June 1940	January 1941	December 1941	December 1942	December 1943	July 1944
Guns	106,400	102,280	52,865	96,415	190,809	249,080
Machine guns	4,400	7,770	3,424	10,716	15,704	24,141
Mortars	1,165	1,073	207	2,360	1,290*	9,225
Artillery	294	317	103	523	962	1,554
Tanks & armoured vehicle	121	310	378	760	1,229	1,669
Operational aircraft	675	1,040	978	1,548	1,734	4,219

* Down due to their replacement by multiple mortars.

Furthermore Hitler launched the production of new secret weapons on which he was relying to win the war after repulsing the landing expected some time in 1944. These were the V.-I and V.-2 rockets and fast pocket submarines capable of staying for long periods underwater.

The effects of the Allied bombing campaign were not so much on the overall rate of German production as through strikes, often based on extremely precise intelligence reports, on factories producing specific items of vital importance.

Thus a raid on Hamburg carried out in November 1943 destroyed the only chemical manufacturing installation capable of producing one of the components of the fuel required to power the Messerschmitt-163 jet fighters, already being turned out at a rate of 80 a month, and production had to be stopped. The absence of this aircraft, which was to have represented a considerable advance, was an important factor in Allied air supremacy in 1944.

Likewise, the bombardment of Peenemunde in 1943 and launching sites under construction in December 1943, considerably delayed the development, production and utilisation of the V.-1.

The conquest of Italy and her airfields put the Romanian oilfields within striking distance enabling their output to be reduced.

On the other hand, the effectiveness of massive Allied bombing in 1943 was only limited. British bombing raids took place by night and therefore lacked in precision. The American attacks were carried out in daylight and turned out too costly in the absence of long-range fighters to escort them, a drawback that was not remedied until 1944. A raid carried out in October 1943 on the Schweinfurt ball-bearing factory in Bavaria by 228 unescorted bombers cost 62 planes destroyed, 138 damaged and the lives of 599 airmen.

APPENDIX 3
DIEPPE AND COMMANDO OPERATIONS IN EUROPE

The decision to execute the Dieppe raid was taken at what was for the Allies a critical moment of the war.

In May 1942, the great victory at Midway, the first Allied victory of strategic importance, inflicted the first severe check on the Axis, hitherto victorious in all theatres since Hitler's accession to power in 1933.

The time therefore seemed ripe for the second strategic confrontation, this time the final offensive battle, the opening of the second front in Europe, called for by Stalin for the last year, decided upon by Roosevelt months before, and anticipated by Churchill back in July 1940. In fact, the conditions required for success had still not all been attained. German strength had not been sufficiently weakened, the build-up of American forces in England had been delayed by German U-boat successes in the Atlantic; there was also the British failure in North Africa (the fall of Tobruk), the continued presence of numerous naval forces in the Pacific, in spite of the victory of Midway against Japan's southward advance. Opening the second front on the Continent in 1942 was clearly not a feasible proposition. What was there to be done?

The Torch landing in French North Africa offered many advantages: it would clear up the situation in French North Africa and the Middle East, remove the threat of the Germans linking up with the Japanese in the Indian Ocean, ease German pressure on the U.S.S.R. by obliging Hitler to recall forces from the east in order to face threats from the south and west. To intensify relief for the Soviet Union and the threat from the west, it was decided, somewhat rashly, not to wait until the summer and Torch to launch an operation limited in resources and time against the continent: Dieppe.

British Combined Operations Command very quickly mounted this operation executed by Canadian forces. Although costly in human lives, the result of the operation was to oblige Hitler to maintain forces in large numbers in the west, while the battle was unfolding in North Africa, and he was needing all available forces in the east to launch his offensive towards the Caucasus with its much needed oil. Dieppe then Torch would contribute to the German defeat before Stalingrad. In addition, the apparent reverse at Dieppe would reinforce the German High Command's over-confidence in its system of coastal defences, and an erroneous belief in the Pas-de-Calais being the likely future Allied landing zone.

The Dieppe raid in August 1942 was the biggest and best known "tip and run" raid on the Continent. But many other commando raids were mounted before Overlord. These were as follows:

- 23-24 June 1940: Boulogne - Le Touquet. 110 men led by Major Tod.
- 14-15 July 1940: Guernesey.
- 3 March 1941: Lofoten (Norway).
- 3 September 1941: Spilsberg.
- 27 December 1941: Vagsoy (Norway). A landing that worried Hitler to the point of keeping on troops in Norway in considerable numbers.
- 27-28 February 1942: Bruneval (France).
- 28 March 1942: Saint-Nazaire.
- 11-12 April 1942: Boulogne.
- 14-15 August 1942: cap Barfleur.
- 18-19 August 1942: Dieppe.
- 2-3 September 1942: Le Casquet lighthouse.
- 7-8 September 1942: near Bayonne.
- 3-4 October 1942: island of Sark.

APPENDIX 4

TABLE OF THE MAIN EVENTS
LEADING UP TO THE LANDING IN EUROPE

(until General Eisenhower took over command)

Preparation June 1940 to January 1944

DATES	EVENTS	COMMENTAIRES
4 June 1940	End of the evacuation of Dunkirk	250,000 British soldiers manage to get back to England where they provide "the nucleus of the future British army" to resist and conquer Nazi Germany.
22 June 1940		Hitler declares: "England has been driven from the continent for ever".
23 June 1940	First British commando operation on the continent	120 British commandos carry out a rapid reconnaissance mission near Boulogne.
July 1940	Creation of a British *Combined Operations Command*	Mission: to prepare the return to the continent, and examine possible raids on the coasts of Europe.
August 1940	Battle of Britain	The Germans bomb England (air defences, means of communication, industrial and coastal installations) in preparation for an invasion.
5 September 1940	Exchange agreement between Great Britain and the United States	50 destroyers lent to Great Britain in exchange for the use of 7 bases on the western Atlantic perimeter.
17 September 1940	Hitler cancels his plans to invade England	Hitler decides to attack Russia on 1 May 1941 so as to be finished before the onset of winter, and then force England to negotiate.
5 November 1940		Presidential Elections in the United States (Roosevelt is re-elected).
January 1941	Meeting between British and American Chiefs of Staff	On the occasion of American supplies to England, top secret talks are held between American and British officers with a view to coming to a common operational strategy. It is agreed that if the United States are drawn into the war and if it spreads to European, Atlantic and Pacific theatres, Hitler is to be defeated first.
March 1941	*Lend-Lease* Bill	The "*Cash and Carry*" system between the United States and Britain is replaced by a financial facility agreement that turns out to be a real aid in Britain's struggle against Germany and to which convoy, repair and other facilities are added.
21 June 1941	German attack on the U.S.S.R.	German armies penetrate into the U.S.S.R. Soviet surprise was complete in spite of warnings given to Stalin by Churchill, who was informed of German projects through channels now known to have been reliable (German coded messages deciphered), but which Stalin did not believe.
July 1941	Material assistance to the U.S.S.R. to fight	The United States and Britain offer material support to the U.S.S.R. in spite of shipping problems, and Britain's own needs.
18 July 1941	First letter from Stalin to Churchill	Stalin acknowledges receipt of assistance offered and expresses the wish that a second front be opened in the west.
9-12 August 1941	**First Roosevelt-Churchill meeting**	Meeting held at Placentia Bay (Newfoundland): – approval of the Atlantic Charter (destruction of the Nazi tyranny); – common message to Stalin; – examination of the situation: Europe (Spain), Far East (Japan), help for Russia, the Middle East and Africa.
7 December 1941	Pearl Harbor Bombing of Singapore and Hong Kong	Japanese surprise attack against the United States.

8 December 1941		The United States declares war on Japan
11 December 1941		Germany and Italy declare war on the United States.
du 22 December au 28 December 1941	"Arcadia" Conference in Washington	Meeting between Churchill, Roosevelt and their Chiefs of Staff: – signature of the United Nations pact, making reference to the Atlantic Charter (of 12 August 1941) whose object is the destruction of Nazi tyranny; – confirmation of first priority given to Germany as war objective. Victory over Japan would follow; – creation of *Combined Chief of Staff* or "meeting of British and American Chiefs of Staff for the direction of the war" with a permanent office in Washington.
April 1942	Chiefs of Staff Conference in London	Harry Hopkins, an adviser to President Roosevelt, General Marshall, U.S. Army Chief of Staff, accompanied by General Wedemeyer, responsible for planning, go on a mission to London to study plans for a return to Europe and the build-up of American troops in Britain to take part in the struggle in Europe.
June 1942	Churchill-Roosevelt Conference in the United States	Observes the impossibility of opening a second front in Europe in 1942 due to inadequate resources; the fall of Tobruk and difficulties in the Middle East bring about a decision for an operation in North Africa (*Torch*) – a crisis atmosphere fortunately tempered by the brilliant American naval victory at **Midway** - the **first severe check** after a string of Axis victories. Roosevelt maintains priority given to the defeat of Germany. During the first half of 1942, Allied naval losses in the Atlantic were heavy, with a peak in June (825,000 tons) making war supplies to Britain, and the build-up of American forces in Britain very difficult.
8 November 1942	*Torch*	Allied landing in French North Africa (Algeria, Morocco). Beginning of the Tunisian campaign against the Germans.
January 1943	Casablanca conference	Churchill and Roosevelt meet, accompanied by their Chiefs of Staff. Combined Chiefs of Staff meeting. Decisions taken: – pursuit of Mediterranean operations (Sicily, possibly Italy) in 1943; a Chief of Staff named COSSAC set up to prepare the return to Europe; – to achieve **preliminary conditions** to entry into the **mainland of Europe**; – mastery of the seas in the Atlantic; – reduction of German industrial and military potential through an **air offensive**; – air supremacy in Europe.
13 April 1943	C.O.S.S.A.C. (*Chief of Staff to the Supreme Allied Commender*)	British General designated: General Morgan (working in London) under direct orders of *Combined Chief of Staff* (C.C.S.). Start of detailed planning for the landing operation.
2nd fortnight of May	*Trident*	C.C.S. meeting to examine plans prepared by COSSAC.
August 1943	Conférence *Quadrant* à Québec	Roosevelt-Churchill get-together and C.C.S. meeting: – plans drawn up by COSSAC approved; – COSSAC detailed to proceed with measures to implement the approved plan.
October 1943	Moscow	Meeting of Soviet, American and British Foreign Affairs ministers to coordinate operations in 1944.
28 November 1943	Meeting of Allied leaders at Tehran	Stalin, Roosevelt and Churchill meet for the first time. Decision to open the second front in May 1944. Stalin requests that the Interallied Commander for the invasion to be named.
6 December 1943	S.H.A.E.F. (*Supreme Headquarters Allied Expeditionnary Forces*	**General Eisenhower appointed Supreme Allied Commander-in-Chief Allied Forces (made public on 25 December).**
15 janvier 1944		**Eisenhower takes up command in London.**

APPENDIX 5

DIRECTIVE TO SUPREME COMMANDER, ALLIED EXPEDITIONARY FORCE

(dated 12 February 1944)

« 1. You are hereby designated as Supreme Allied Commander of the forces placed under your orders for operations of liberation of Europe from Germans. Your title will be Supreme Commander, Allied Expeditionary Force.

2. Task. You will enter the continent of Europe and, in conjunction with the other United Nations, undertake operations aimed at the heart of Germany and the destruction of her armed forces. The date for entering the continent is the month of May, 1944. After adequate Channel ports have been secured, exploitation will be directed towards securing an area that will facilitate both ground and air operations against the enemy.

3. Notwithstanding the target date above, you will be prepared at any time to take immediate advantage of favourable circumstances such as withdrawal by the enemy on your front, to effect a re-entry into the Continent with such forces as you have available at the time; a general plan for this operation when approved will be furnished for your assistance.

4. Command. You are responsible to the Combined Chiefs of Staff and will exercise command generally in accordance with the diagram at Appendix [reproduced on page 67]. Direct communication with the United States and British American Chiefs of Staff is authorized in the interest of facilitating your operations and for arranging necessary logistic support.

5. Logistics. In the United Kingdom the responsibility for logistics organization, concentration, movement and supply of forces to meet the requirements of your plan will rest with British Service Ministries so far as British forces are concerned. So far as American forces are concerned, this responsibility will rest with the United States War and Navy Departments. You will be responsible for the coordination of logistical arrangements on the continent. You will also be responsible for coordinating the requirements of British and United States forces under your command.

6. Coordination of operations of other Forces and Agencies. In preparation for your assault on enemy occupied Europe, Sea and Air Forces Agencies of sabotage, subversion and propaganda, acting under a variety of authorities are now in action. You may recommend any variation in these activities which may seem to you desirable.

7. Relationship to United Nations Forces in other areas. Responsibility will rest with the Combined Chiefs of Staff for supplying information relating to operations of the Forces of the U.S.S.R. for your guidance in timing your operations. It is understood that the Soviet Forces will launch an offensive at about the same time as Overlord with the object of preventing the German forces from transferring from the Eastern to the Western front. The Allied Commander in Chief, Mediterranean Theater, will conduct operations designed to assist your operation, including the launching of an attack against the south of France at about the same time as Overlord. The Combined Chiefs of Staff will place under your command the forces operating in Southern France as soon as you are in a position to assume such command. You will submit timely recommendations compatible with this regard.

8. Relationship with Allied Governments. The re-establishment of Civil Governments and Liberated Allied Territories and the administration of enemy territories. Further instructions will be issued to you on these subjects at a later date. "

CHAIN OF COMMAND

```
  U.S Chiefs of Staff              Combined              British Chiefs of Staff
                                Chiefs of Staff
                                       |
                          Supreme commander of the
                          allied expeditionary forces
                                       |
                     Supreme Commander - 2nd in command
                                       |
                                 Chief of Staff
                                       |
                            Combined Chief of Staff
                                       |
   ┌───────────────────┬──────────────┴──────────────┬───────────────────────┐
 Chief           Commander-              Commander-            Commander -
 of the Allied   U.S. Army              British Army          Chief of the Allied
 naval forces    group                   group               Expeditionary Air forces
   ┌──────────────┐                      ┌─────────────────────┐
U.S. Naval      British Naval        U.S. Tactical          British Tactical
Forces          Forces               Air Forces             Air Forces
```

NB: The strategic U.S. air forces in Europe and British Bomber Command came under the command of the Combined Chief of Staff.

APPENDIX 6

GERMAN DIVISIONS COMMITTED IN NORMANDY

Date engaged	Division	from
Initially 6 June	91st Division 352nd Division 716th Division 243rd Division 5th Parachute Division (detached regiment) 21st Panzer 709th Division (at Cherbourg)	
7 June	12th S.S. Panzer	Evreux
8 June	Panzer Lehr 353rd Division	Le Mans Morlaix
10 June	3rd Parachute	Brest
11 June	77th Division 17th S.S. Panzer Grenadier	Saint-Malo Poitiers
13 June	2nd Panzer	Abbeville
15 June	16th Luftwaffe Feldsdivision	Hollande
18 June	1st S.S. Panzer	Belgique
23 June	2nd S.S. Panzer Corps Command	Poland
25 June	9th S.S. Panzer 10th S.S. Panzer	Poland
28 June	2nd S.S.Panzer (alerted on 7 June)	Toulouse
29 June	346th Division 711st Division	Between Caen and the Seine, adjoining Seventh
	276th Division 277th Division	Basque Country Narbonne

By the end of June, the 9 panzer divisions committed (1st S.S., 9th S.S., 10th S.S., 12th S.S., Panzer Lehr, 2nd, 21st, 2nd S.S., 17th Panzer Grenadier) had already lost 350 tanks.

Date engaged	Division	from
20 July	116th Panzer	North of the Seine, from Nantes
24 July	271st Division 272nd Division	Nîmes Narbonne
30 July	84th Division 326th Division 331st Division 708th Division 363rd Division	North of Rouen Pas-de-Calais Pas-de-Calais La Rochelle Denmark
from 1 to 5 August	265th Division 343rd Division 266th Division 276th Division	Committed on the spot in Brittany (Brest, Lorient, Vannes)
from 4 to 6 August	9th Panzer	Avignon
6 August	89th Division 85th Division	Norway Abbeville
15 August	48th Division 17th Luftwaffe Feldsdivision 344th Division 338th Division	Ostende Nord, Le Havre Le Touquet Marseille

The total number of divisions committed in Normandy was 42, including 11 armoured (panzer divisions). 1 further division was blocked in the Channel Islands.

Until the end of July, no elements were drawn from Fifteenth Army (except for a battalion of Tiger tanks) under the illusion that it had to be kept in reserve to face a second invasion. After 20 July, 7 divisions were directed south of the Seine.

APPENDIX 7

PART PLAYED BY THE FRENCH IN THE BATTLE OF NORMANDY

The story of the battle of Normandy as described herein is strictly military, tactical and strategic, and pays no detailed attention to the operational activities of the French within an overall picture that was essentially the work of the American and British forces.

It should however be remembered that French units did take part in this victory:
– 1st Naval Rifle Commando Battalion of Commandant Kieffer which landed at Ouistreham on 6 June;
– naval forces;
   – off *Juno*:
      • the destroyer *La Combattante*,
      • the frigate *La Découverte*,
      • the corvette *D'Estienne-d'Orves* ;
   – off *Utah*:
      • the corvettes *Aconit* and *Renoncule* ;
   – off *Omaha*:
      • the cruisers *Georges-Leygues* and *Montcalm*,
      • the corvette *Roselys*,
      • the frigates *L'Escarmouche* and *L'Aventure*;
   – off *Gold*:
      • the corvette *La Surprise*;

– air forces:
      • fighter flights *Alsace 3/2*, *Île-de-France 4/2*, *Cigognes 1/2* and *Berry 2/2*,
      • the light bomber group *Lorraine 1/20*,
      • the heavy bomber group *Guyenne 2/23* and *Tunisie 1/25* ;
– Commandant Bourgoin's 2nd parachute battalion, whose sticks of pathfinders in the night of 5 to 6 June have been mentioned;
– General Leclerc's 2nd Armoured Division brought ashore at *Utah* on 1 August and which operated within the American Third Army.

Obviously we must not forget the role of the Resistance, a vital one in the area of intelligence prior to the landing and whose coordinated efforts with the Jedburgh teams considerably hampered the arrival of German reinforcements. Some have been mentioned in the course of the present account: Brittany, eastern France, the southwest, etc. Special mention has been made of delays to 2nd S.S. Panzer, coming from Toulouse, and to 9th and 10th S.S. Panzer, coming from Poland.

General de Gaulle set foot once again on French soil on 14 June, and restored the French administration at Bayeux that same day.

BIBLIOGRAPHY

Books dealing with the battle of Normandy are too numerous to be able to indicate them all. Among the numerous volumes on the subject, only some that are required reading for anyone wishing to understand the place of the battle of Normandy in the Second World War are mentioned herer.

• Wilmot (Chester), *The Struggle for Europe*, Collins, Sons and Co, London, 1952
• Churchill (sir Winston Leonard Spencer), *The Second World War*, London, Cassel, 1948-1952. vol. 1, chap. V.
• Morgan (Sir Frederick, Lieutenant-General), *Overture to Overlord*, London, Hodder and Stoughton, 1950.

• Bryant (Arthur), *The Turn of the Tide*, Collins, Sons and Co, 1958. – *Triumph in the West*, Collins, Sons and Co, 1960.
• Eisenhower (Dwight David, General), *Report by the Supreme Commander to the Combined Chiefs of Staff on the Operations in Europe of the Allied Expeditionary Forces His Majesty's Stationery Office*, 1946
• Liddell Hart (B. H.), The German Generals Talk, New York, Morrow1948.

• Cave Brown (Antony), *Bodyguard of lies*, W.H. Allen and Co Ltd, 1976.
• Rapport officiel, *Victory in the West*, Her Majesty's Stationnery Office, 1962.
• Wedemeyer (Albert C.), *Wedemeyer Reports*.
• Compagnon (J., General), *Normandie 44: victoire stratégique*, Revue historique des Armées, 1979, n° 2.

TABLE OF CONTENTS

Glossary of abbreviations:

USIS: United States Information Service - IWM: Imperial War Museum ECPA: Établissement Cinéma Photo des Armées. - R.H.A.: Revue Historique des Armées.

Map graphics: Patrick Mérienne

Acknowledgements:
• Colonel Legout, curator of the Musée du Débarquement at Arromanches, for providing documentation featured on the following pages 24, 79, 80 (h), 89 (mg), 95 (b), 98 (g), 101, 102 (hd), 117 (h), 121, 139 (hd et b).
• Dr. Jean-Pierre Bénamou, O.B.E., M.S.V., curator of the Musée de la Bataille de Normandie in Bayeux, for providing documentation featured on the following pages 14 (g), 15 (h), 17 (h), 18, 26, 29 (b), 30, 34, 35, 36, 37, 38, 39 (b), 41 (h et b), 42, 44, 46 (h et b), 47, 48, 49, 50,53, 60, 62 (m), 62 (b), 63 (h and b), 64, 73 (h), 78 (h and b), 84 (m et b), 85 (g et d), 89 (hd and bd), 91 (hd), 94 (h), 100 (hg), 102 (b), 108, 112 (h), 126 (b), 127, 132 (b), 133 (d), 137 (hd et g), 140 (b), 151.
• Tanguy Le Sant: document on page 83 (b).
• Philippe Pique, éditions Orep : Maps and graphics pages 61, 90, 130 (Studio Vert).

2001, 2007, Éditions Ouest-France – Edilarge SA. Rennes
Printed by MAME Imprimeurs – Tours (37)
ISBN 978.2.7373.4269.1 – Copyright registration : February 2001 – Publisher No : 5454.02.15.03.08
www.editionsouestfrance.fr